EDUCATING
FOR
WISDOM
AND
COMPASSION

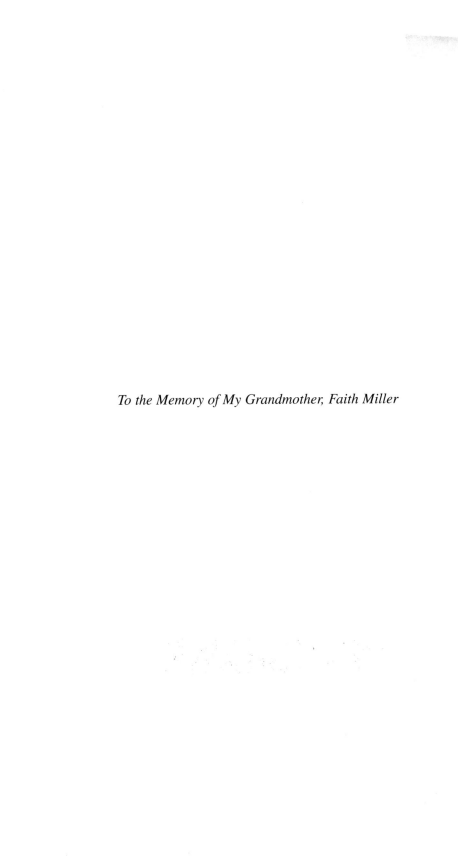

To the Memory of My Grandmother, Faith Miller

EDUCATING
FOR
WISDOM
AND
COMPASSION

CREATING CONDITIONS
FOR TIMELESS LEARNING

John P. Miller

CORWIN PRESS
A SAGE Publications Company
Thousand Oaks, California

For information:

Corwin Press
A Sage Publications Company
2455 Teller Road
Thousand Oaks, California 91320
www.corwinpress.com

Sage Publications Ltd.
1 Oliver's Yard
55 City Road
London EC1Y 1SP
United Kingdom

Sage Publications India Pvt. Ltd.
B-42, Panchsheel Enclave
Post Box 4109
New Delhi 110 017 India

Printed in the United States of America

Library of Congress Cataloging-in-Publication Data

Miller, John P., 1943–
Educating for wisdom and compassion: Creating conditions for
timeless learning/John P. Miller
    p. cm.
Includes bibliogrphical references and index
ISBN 1–4129–1703–4 (cloth)—ISBN 1–4129–1704–2 (pbk.)
    1. Education, Humanistic. 2. Meditation. 3. Holistic education. I. Title
LC1011.M54 2006
370.112—dc22   2005008044

This book is printed on acid-free paper.

05   06   07   08   09   10   9   8   7   6   5   4   3   2   1

Acquisitions Editor:	Faye Zucker
Editorial Assistant:	Gem Rabanera
Production Editor:	Beth A. Bernstein
Copy Editor:	Cate Huisman
Typesetter:	C&M Digitals (P) Ltd.
Proofreader:	Joyce Li
Indexer:	Judy Hunt
Cover Designer:	Rose Storey

Contents

Acknowledgments

A book reflects many connections. I am grateful to the Ontario Institute for Studies in Education at the University of Toronto for providing the six-month study leave to work on this book. Thanks also to the students whom I work with at OISE/UT. Many of the examples of timeless learning in this book come from them. These students are experienced teachers working on graduate degrees in education and bring a wealth of experience and insight to my classes.

Thank you to my colleagues at OISE/UT and the Spirituality in Education Network who have offered both inspiration and support to my efforts. Lourdes Arguelles and Bob London who are members of the network were kind enough to provide helpful feedback to the publisher. I appreciate very much that Aline Wolf took the time to go over the Montessori section. Thanks to Tobin Hart and David Marshak who read the completed manuscript and made suggestions for the final revisions. To Ron Miller, thanks again for your willingness to read and comment on my work.

I have been practicing meditation for 30 years and I have had several teachers who have had a profound impact on my own practice and indirectly this book. They include Joseph Goldstein, Jack Kornfield, Sharon Salzberg, Christopher Titmus, and most recently, Molly Swan and Norman Feldman.

At Corwin Press I would like to thank Beth Bernstein who oversaw the production process and Cate Huisman who did the copy editing. I am particularly grateful to Faye Zucker who guided the book through the initial editorial phase. Her support and guidance have been instrumental to the publication of the book. Thanks also to her assistant, Gem Rabanera.

Finally I thank my wife, Midori, who embodies many of the qualities described in these pages.

Corwin Press gratefully acknowledges the contributions of the following reviewers:

Lourdes Arguelles
Professor of Education and Cultural Studies
Claremont Graduate University
Claremont, CA

Geoffrey Caine
Learning and Education Consultant
Caine Learning L.L.C.
Idyllwild, CA

Tobin Hart
Associate Professor
Department of Psychology
State University of West Georgia
Carrollton, GA

Robert London
Professor
College of Education,
California State University at San Bernardino
San Bernardino, CA

David Marshak
Professor of Education
Seattle University
Seattle, WA

Pearl Solomon
Associate Professor of Teacher Education
St. Thomas Aquinas College
Sparkill, NY

COPYRIGHT ACKNOWLEDGMENTS

First four lines on page 48, used as epigraph, from *Tao Te Ching by Lao Tzu, A New English Version, With Foreword and Notes*, by Stephen Mitchell. Translation copyright © 1988 by Stephen Mitchell. Reprinted by permission of Harper Collins.

"Just One Minute" by Naomi Baer © 2003 by Inquiring Mind. Reprinted by permission of *Inquiring Mind: The Semiannual Journal of the Vipassana Community,* Volume 20, Number 1 (Fall 2003). For more information please visit www.inquiringmind.com, or write to Inquiring Mind, P.O. Box 9999, Berkeley, CA 94709.

Extracts from *School with Forest and Meadow* (1995), by Ikue Tezuka, published by Caddo Gap Press. Reprinted with permission from Ikue Tezuka.

Selection on daily life of mindful teacher reprinted by permission of Astrid De Cairos.

Certain portions of this book have been adapted from previously published journal articles. These include:

Section on transcendental education from "Emerson, Thoreau and Alcott: Prophets of Holistic Education," in *Nurturing Our Wholeness: Perspectives on Spirituality in Education* (2002), John P. Miller and Yoshiharu Nakagawa (Eds.). Reprinted with permission of The Foundation for Educational Renewal and Holistic Education Press; www.great-ideas.org

Section on Krishnamurti from "Krishnamurti and Holistic Education" in *Encounter: Education for Meaning and Social Justice* (2000), Volume 13, Number 4, pages 36–44. Reprinted with permission of Holistic Education Press; www.great-ideas.org

Section on author's research from "Meditating Teachers: A Qualitative Study" coauthor Ayako Nozawa, in the *Journal of In-Service Education* (2002), Volume 28, Number 1, pages 179–192. Reprinted with permission from the *Journal of In-Service Education.*

About the Author

 **John P. (Jack) Miller, PhD,** is professor in the Department of Curriculum, Teaching, and Learning at the Ontario Institute for Studies in Education (OISE) at the University of Toronto and Head of OISE's Centre for Teacher Development. He has also been visiting professor at Shinwa Women's University in Kobe, Japan, and at Rietsumeiken University in Kyoto, Japan. Professor Miller teaches courses in holistic education and spirituality in education. He has also led workshops and given keynote addresses on those topics at conferences around the world.

Notable among his many books, chapters, and journal articles are *Holistic Learning and Spirituality in Education: Breaking New Ground* (2004), *Education and the Soul: Toward a Spiritual Curriculum* (2000), *The Contemplative Practitioner* (1994), *Holistic Learning: The Teacher's Guide to Integrated Studies* (1990), *Curriculum: Perspectives and Practice* (1985), *The Holistic Curriculum* (1988), *The Compassionate Teacher* (1981), and *Humanizing the Classroom* (1976).

PART I

Timeless Learning: Definitions and Fundamentals

CHAPTER ONE

Timeless Learning

In the pursuit of knowledge, every day something is added.
In the pursuit of the Tao, every day something is dropped.

—Lao-tzu

S piritual traditions can provide a unique perspective on learning;
a perspective that has been overlooked in our approaches
to education. For many educators learning involves "adding" or accumulating knowledge. Critically named the "banking" approach to
learning, this method requires students to memorize and retain knowledge. This approach is almost always assessed by paper-and-pencil
tests. A current rendition of "adding knowledge" is Hirsch's (Hirsch,
Kett, and Trefil, 1988) *The Dictionary of Cultural Literacy.* Hirsch
argues that students need to acquire specific information in order to
be successful in the world. This shared information is also important
in "holding together the social fabric of the nation" (p. xi). Hirsch
also suggests that the development of such skills as reading are
closely related to how much a student knows. He states: "An important key to solving the twin problems of learning and literacy is to
attain the broadly shared background knowledge I have called 'cultural literacy'"(p. xiii). Hirsch endorses what "Ernest Gellner calls
school-transmitted cultures" (p. xiv). Acquiring knowledge is at the
heart of the transmission orientation. This orientation tends to see
learners as passive as they absorb information from the teacher and
textbook.

Transmission has a role in learning but needs to be complemented
by what I call *timeless learning*.

WHAT IS TIMELESS LEARNING?

When it comes to defining time, only the oceanic need apply—the Montaignes or Joyces, Shakespeares or Rousseaus, eastern philosophers or children. They know their now, they know the really wild vibe of the present is this; now is the only time when the moment can meet the eternal- and they know that moment is momentous (Griffiths, 1999, p. 36).

Most of us have had the experience of the timeless moment. We feel we are in unbounded space. It is in timeless moments when powerful learning occurs. The way that Helen Keller first learned hand sign language from her teacher, Annie Sullivan, is an example of timeless learning. Annie put Helen's hand under the water coming from the pump and at the same time her fingers tapped out the word "water." In that one moment the world opened to Helen. Helen's story is well known. Below is another good example of timeless learning as Helen wrote about being present in the moment through nature:

Hear the music of voices, the song of a bird, the mighty strains of an orchestra as if you would be stricken deaf tomorrow.

Touch each object as if tomorrow your tactile sense would fail.

Smell the perfume of flowers, taste with relish each morsel, as if tomorrow you could never taste or smell again.

Make the most of every sense.

Glory in all the facets and pleasures and beauty which the world reveals to you. (cited in Goleman, Kaufman, and Ray, 1992, p. 174)

In the timeless learning our experience becomes much more immediate. We are not thinking of the past or the future. Wittgenstein said "Only the man who lives not in time but in the present is happy" (cited in Griffiths, 1999, p. 33). One of the teachers in my class commented that after practicing being more in the moment the students told her that she seemed happier.

As a teacher, I have become more aware of my students and their feelings in the class. Instead of rushing through the day's events, I take the time to enjoy our day's experiences and opportune moments. The students have commented that I seem happier. I do tend to laugh more and I think it is because I am more aware, alert and "present," instead of thinking about what I still need to do (Miller, 1995, p. 22).

Let's turn now to the examining the characteristics of timeless learning.

WHAT ARE THE CHARACTERISTICS OF TIMELESS LEARNING?

Timeless learning is multidimensional and includes a variety of characteristics. Although a specific experience of timeless learning would not necessarily include all of the characteristics outlined below, these characteristics are the most often linked with the learning experiences described in this book.

Holistic/Integrative

Timeless learning is not limited to the intellect; it also is connected to the emotions, the body, and soul/spirit. *Soul/spirit* is defined here as a vital, mysterious energy that can give meaning and purpose to our lives. Timeless learning recognizes that all these elements are linked interdependently. For example, if I have an insight or idea, it can quicken the heartbeat which again affects the rhythms in the body. One description of timeless learning comes from a student who describes his experience in meditation:

> The session began with many thoughts and physical sensations, which quickly settled down and although they didn't totally disappear, were not much in my awareness afterward. It was a very quiet and uneventful meditation with the mantra barely present. In fact, there was not much present at all except the awareness of myself just being there. This continued until towards the end of the session when I began to have certain feelings or knowledge; it's hard to explain how the two combine into one. It's like you know something with every cell of your body, to the point that you actually feel it everywhere. . . . I was keenly aware that I was part of all that was around me. There was no distinction between my inner self, my body, and my surroundings. This awareness extended out so that I felt a part of all that there is. As I read what I'm writing, the words sound grandiose, whereas

the experience was very simple. However, it was also profound, peaceful and fulfilling at all levels; physical, intellectual, and spiritual. (Miller, 1994, p. 130)

This example of timeless learning had an impact on the intellect, the body, emotions, and spirit.

Timeless learning also is integrative in that it tends to link the different parts of ourselves. Too often we compartmentalize learning into different aspects such as the intellect and the physical and they are left separate. In timeless learning they are seen as connected.

Embodied

Timeless learning does not just remain in the head; it becomes embodied. This aspect is related to the integration just described in that the person begins to live what is learned. What many people find so inspiring about Gandhi and Martin Luther King is the way they embodied their own teachings. They were living examples of nonviolent action and protest. It was exactly this embodiment of their teachings that inspired their followers. Stanley Wolpert (2001) makes this point in his biography of Gandhi:

By re-creating himself, through the power of his passion, in the humble, vulnerable image of India's poorest starving naked millions, Gandhi could, when moved to do so by his "inner voice," call upon that unarmed ragged army, whose pain he mirrored and magnified in his own naked body, to follow him barefoot up India's Via Dolorosa to freedom. And countless millions unhesitatingly did follow him, not as a modern political leader, nor as a medieval native prince or martial maharaja, but as their own Mahatma, India's "Great Soul," the only title he ever enjoyed, until even that became too burdensome and honorific for his passionate spirit. (pp. 4–5)

Gandhi himself summed up this point so well when he said: "My life is my message."

As teachers we need to embody qualities that are conducive to timeless learning such as caring, mindful presence, and conveying a sense of respect to the student. Carl Rogers (1969) identified some of these characteristics in his work as he identified empathy, respect, and genuineness as key factors in the success of teachers.

Embodiment does not mean sainthood or striving to be perfect. Rather there is simply the desire to live in a way that is congruent with our expressed beliefs. It is this congruency that leads to embodiment.

Connected

Timeless learning connects. First there is the connection to various aspects of ourselves (e.g., intellect, emotions, soul, and body) which involves the integrative dimension that was mentioned earlier. Second there is the connection to others. In timeless learning the sense of separate self tends to lessen and we see ourselves in relationship to others. A natural sense of compassion arises as we realize how other beings desire much of what we desire (e.g., health and happiness). Connecting to others leads to a communion and community. Communion occurs when the souls of two people connect with each other. Community involves more than just two people experiencing connection to a much larger group.

Another connection that can arise is our link to the earth. Timeless learning often leads to sense of how we are supported and nourished by the earth. Indigenous peoples have felt this connection and reading their literature can help restore the connection in ourselves. Finally, timeless learning connects us to the cosmos as a whole. This last connection can deepen our connection to the mystery of being in the universe.

Connectedness is an extremely important aspect of timeless learning. Sometimes people involved in spiritual practice can pursue a path that leads to solipsism. Instead of being connected to others the person can feel separate and sometimes superior to others. Cults, or cultish behavior, can also arise from this false sense of separation. The ego subtly uses spiritual practices such as meditation to differentiate oneself from others and to see oneself as more "evolved." A real test of spiritual practice and timeless learning is the development of deep and lasting compassion.

Soulful

Timeless learning reaches that part of ourselves that Emerson and more recently, Thomas Moore, have called *soul*. Soul is defined as a vital and mysterious energy that can deepen meaning and purpose in life. Timeless learning usually connects with this part of ourselves and can give the student a deeper awareness of his or her place in the larger scheme of things.

How does this happen? Sometimes it can happen through the presence of the teacher which somehow connects with the student's soul. On occasion it can arise through a particular learning experience. For example, reading a poem or story can touch the student's soul. Experiences with the earth such as gardening or caring for an animal can also touch the soul and I have described some of these possibilities in my book, *Education and the Soul* (2000).

I like Emerson's view of how colleges should educate young people:

> Colleges . . . can only highly serve us, when they aim not to drill, but to create; when they gather from far every ray of various genius to their hospitable halls, and, by the concentrated fires, set the hearts of their youth on flame. (from "The American Scholar," an oration delivered before the Phi Beta Kappa Society at Cambridge, August 31, 1837).

"Setting the hearts of their youth on flame" is another way of describing touching the soul. It moves education beyond just acquiring skills to a level that again touches every aspect of the student's being.

Transformative

Timeless learning can lead to profound change in the individual. John Gerber offers the following definition: "Transformative learning (for me) is a process of personal and community growth toward a state of egolessness and communion" (Zajonc, 2003, p. 16). Gerber emphasizes how timeless learning leads toward the connectedness described earlier.

Although timeless learning can be transformative, there is certainly no guarantee when, how, or under what conditions the transformation will occur. Some transformation can be incremental; other changes can be monumental.

One of my favorite examples of transformation comes from Satish Kumar. Satish has spent much of his life walking. His first walk was a halfway around the world for peace. He describes the experience and transformation that occurred:

In wandering I felt a sense of union with the whole sky, the infinite earth and sea. I felt myself a part of the cosmic existence. It was as if by walking I was making love to the earth itself. Wandering was my path, my true self, my true being. It released my soul-force; it brought me in relation to everything else. (Kumar, 1999, p. 100)

Transformation can also come through suffering. Thomas Moore (2002) makes the point that the spiritual teachers that he trusts have been people who have often dealt with difficulty in their lives. He says: "Some of the best priests I know are homosexual; they have struggled with themselves in a fearful, phobic and unaccepting culture" (p. 78).

Flow

Timeless learning is often characterized by what Csikszentmihalyi has called the *flow* experience. Flow occurs when a person becomes fully immersed in an experience. Csikszentmihalyi (1997) gives the example of someone skiing:

Imagine, for instance, that you are skiing down a slope and your full attention is focused on the movements of your body, the position of the skis, the air whistling past your face, and the snow shrouded trees running by. There is no room in your awareness for conflicts and contradictions; you know that distracting thought or emotion might get you buried facedown in the snow. . . . The run is so perfect that all you want is for it to last forever, to immerse yourself completely in the experience. (p. 29)

Flow experiences usually give immediate feedback to people so that they can react quickly to the situation. The situation itself is usually challenging but not so challenging that success is clearly not possible. These challenges call on people to focus their attention completely. It is interesting how Csikszentmihalyi describes the experience: "Self-consciousness disappears, yet one feels stronger than usual. The sense of time is distorted: hours seem to pass by in minutes" (1997, p. 31). He makes the direct link to timeless learning.

Csikszentmihalyi also states the state of flow is also optimal for learning. The state of awareness that arises in flow helps the individual in acquiring new perspectives and skills.

Participatory

Timeless learning often occurs in a context where we are participating in the co-creation of knowledge. Ferrer (2002) makes this point: "Participatory refers to role the individual consciousness plays during transpersonal events. This relation is not one of appropriation, possession, or passive representation of knowledge, but of *communion* and *co-creative participation*" (p. 121). Ferrer makes the point that knowing in this way is not restricted to individual experience. It is profoundly relational.

St Basil discusses this type of knowing in a Christian context: "Knowing God occurs by participation in the 'true life . . . returning to the original good.' In this participation God offers 'intimacy,' a result of our 'affective' and 'moral' knowledge of God" (cited by Chirban, 1986, p. 304). The participatory aspect can also be explained by referring to Buber's famous *I-thou* relationship where two or more people encounter one another in an open and free manner. There is no attempt to control the relationship or activity that occurs within the relationship.

Satish Kumar (1999) in encountering another individual seeks the "door" of mutuality even in the most difficult of relationships. One of his teachers explains: "Like that, when I meet a landlord, he has many faults and shortcomings, and his egotism is like a wall. But he has a little door. If you are prepared to find this door, it means you have risen above your own egotism and you enter his heart" (p. 53).

Nondualistic

Timeless learning tends to be nondualistic in that the knower and known become one. Emerson wrote: "A painter told me that nobody could draw a tree without in some sort becoming a tree." He adds: "By deeper apprehension, . . . the artist attains the power of awakening other souls to a given activity" (p. 134). For Emerson, nondual knowing can awaken others. Nondual knowing is also called contemplation which is discussed in more detail in Chapter 6. In contemplation we do not just reflect on something; we merge with the object of contemplation. In timeless learning we find the barrier between ourselves and the world disappearing as distinctions such as inner and outer drop away.

In timeless learning we tend to move back and forth between both forms; it is not a matter of clinging to one (nondualism) and rejecting the other (dualism) but working with both. Dualistic forms of knowing such as reflecting on an experience can allow for assimilation of contemplative experience.

Mysterious and Unexplainable

Timeless learning participates in the grand Mystery of being and the cosmos. There is always some unexplainable and mysterious element to timeless learning that can leave us with a sense of awe and wonder.

Zen and Taoism emphasize this element. For example, Ray Grigg (1994) cites the following Zen saying: "The most dangerous thing in the world is to think you understand something" (p. 247). He then follows with a quotation from Taoism, "Knowing is the way of fools" (p. 247). Both these quotations point to how experience cannot be explained away. Griggs argues that this wisdom leads to a "perpetual preparedness" where the person approaches each situation with a readiness and openness. He states: "Each individual person becomes the balanced and shapeless center of the universe, dancing alone with the unpredictable order that swirls everywhere" (p. 247).

The awareness of the Mystery can lead to a deep sense of humility which can sometimes be lacking in professors, teachers, and academics. A professor who admits to not knowing is looking for trouble; this runs counter to what is expected of academics. Yet when we encounter this quality how refreshing it can be.

It should be noted that this aspect of timeless learning is very difficult to communicate to others. In the words of Robert Blyth:

> To know that there is nothing to know, and to grieve that it is so difficult to communicate this "nothing to know" to others—this is the life of Zen, this is the deepest thing in the world. (cited in Sohl & Carr, 1976, p. 95)

Despite these difficulties in communicating, wisdom can arise from recognizing the Mystery.

Abraham Heschel (1972) wrote:

> A return to reverence is the first prerequisite for a revival of wisdom. . . . Wisdom comes from awe rather than from shrewdness. It is evoked not in moments of calculation but in moments of being in rapport with the mystery of reality. The greatest insights happen to us moments of awe. (p. 72)

Immeasurable

Emerson (1990) wrote that "the results of life are uncalculated and uncalculable" (p. 238). This statement will not please those today obsessed with accountability and testing. Timeless learning cannot be easily measured and certainly not in the short term. Emerson adds: "The years teach much which the days never know" (p. 238). We can try to assess the effects of timeless learning as we reflect on our lives. Techniques such as journal writing, narrative, and autobiography may help here. We certainly should not succumb to trying to reduce the outcomes of timeless learning to conventional research methodologies.

Ferrer (2002) makes the point that one of the major problems with transpersonal approaches is the almost exclusive reliance on the language and methods of empiricism (p. 56). Braud and Anderson (1998) have provided an alternative to the empirical model in their recent work. Techniques such as imagery, art, and what is called "integral inquiry" are suggested as alternatives.

I return to the issue of accountability in the last chapter.

WHAT DOES TIMELESS LEARNING BRING TO TODAY'S CLASSROOMS?

Among the issues we will discuss in the chapters that follow are the benefits timeless learning can bring to today's classrooms and schools. In brief, these benefits include:

- Issues of character. Timeless learning helps students develop deep joy, wholeness, awe and wonder, and a sense of purpose.
- Issues of health. Research on meditation and other contemplative practices continues to show improvements in heart rate, blood pressure, anxiety reduction, and mental health.

- Issues of learning readiness and success. Timeless learning helps students improve their attention, alertness, perception, and memory.

CONCLUSION

Although timeless learning cannot easily be assessed, it is a powerful form of learning. It is the learning that "sticks"; it makes a difference in our lives. Like the meditator describing his experiences at the beginning of this chapter, timeless learning paradoxically can be both simple and profound at the same time. Timeless learning can arise through ordinary and extraordinary events. A simple walk in the woods as described by Keller can, for example, touch us deeply and open us more directly to the natural world.

Education can consist of both timeless and time-bound learning. My argument is that we have given little or no space for the timeless in our education. However, I am not suggesting that our entire focus should be on the timeless. Inevitably learning skills and acquiring some basic knowledge is more time bound. I will address this issue again in Chapter 8.

The philosophical and spiritual foundations of timeless learning are explored in the next chapter with a discussion of the perennial philosophy. In chapters 3–6, four central processes of timeless learning are presented: *letting go, attention, compassion,* and *contemplation.* The next three chapters (7–9) discuss various educational approaches to and examples of timeless learning in both private and public school settings. Finally, the last chapter discusses the outcomes, or fruits, of timeless learning. This chapter includes a discussion of the research on various aspects of timeless learning.

REFERENCES

Braud, W., & Anderson, R. (Eds.). (1998). *Transpersonal research methods for the social sciences: Honoring human experience.* Thousand Oaks, CA: Sage.

Chirban, J. T. (1986). Developmental stages in Eastern Orthodox Christianity. In K. Wilber, J. Engler, & D. Brown (Eds.), *Transformations of consciousness: Conventional and contemplative perspectives on development* (pp. 285–314). Boston: Shambhala.

Csikszentmihalyi, M. (1997). *Finding flow: The psychology of engagement with everyday life.* New York: Basic Books.

Emerson, R. W. (1990). *Selected essays, lectures and poems* (R. D. Richardson, Ed.). New York: Bantam.

Ferrer, J. N. (2002). *Revisioning transpersonal theory: A participatory vision of human spirituality.* Albany, NY: SUNY Press.

Goleman, D., Kaufman, P., & Ray, M. (1992). *The creative spirit.* New York: Dutton.

Griffiths, J. (1999). *A sideways look at time.* New York: Tarcher/Putnam.

Grigg, R. (1994). *The Tao of Zen.* Boston: Charles E. Tuttle.

Heschel, A. J. (1972). *God in search of man.* New York: Octagon.

Hirsch, Jr., E. D., Kett, J. F., & Trefil, J. (1988). *The dictionary of cultural literacy.* Boston: Houghton Mifflin.

Kohlberg, L., & Mayer, R. (1972). Development as an aim of education. *The Harvard Educational Review, 42,* 449–496.

Kumar, S. (1999). *Path without destination.* New York: William Morrow.

Lao-tzu. (1988). *Tao te ching* (S. Mitchell, Trans.). New York: Harper and Row.

Miller, J. (1994). *The contemplative practitioner: Meditation in education and the professions.* Westport, CT: Bergin and Garvey.

Miller, J. (1995). Meditating teachers. *Inquiring Mind, 12,* 19–22.

Miller, J. (2000). *Education and the soul: Toward a spiritual curriculum.* Albany, NY: SUNY Press.

Moore, T. (2002). *The soul's religion: Cultivating a profoundly spiritual way of life.* New York: Harper Collins.

Rogers, C. (1969). *Freedom to learn.* Columbus, OH: Charles Merrill.

Sohl, R., & Carr, A. (Eds.). (1976). *Games Zen masters play: Writings of R. H. Blyth.* New York: Mentor.

Wolpert, S. (2001). *Gandhi's passion: The life and legacy of Mahatma Gandhi.* New York: Oxford University Press.

Zajonc, A. (2003). *Survey of transformative and spiritual dimensions of higher education.* Northampton, MA: The Center for Contemplative Mind in Society.

CHAPTER TWO

The Perennial Philosophy: A Relaxed Universalism

> *I am part of the whole that is governed by nature; . . . I stand in some intimate connection with other kindred parts.*
>
> —Marcus Aurelius

FOUNDATIONS OF THE PERENNIAL PHILOSOPHY

The roots of timeless learning can be found in a core wisdom underlying various spiritual traditions and teachings. This core wisdom is referred to as *the perennial philosophy.* It is possible to identify the perennial philosophy, or at least aspects of the philosophy, within the mystical thread of most religions and spiritual psychologies. The search for the perennial philosophy can be traced to thinkers such as Plotinus and Augustine. The term was first used by Agostino Steuco in referring the work of the Renaissance philosopher, Marsilio Ficino. Leibniz picked up this thread in 18th century. In the last century Aldous Huxley (1970) wrote a book on this topic. His brief definition of the perennial philosophy is:

> the metaphysic that recognizes a divine Reality substantial to the world of things and lives and minds; the psychology that finds in the soul something similar to, or even identical with, divine Reality; the ethic that places man's final end in the knowledge of the immanent and transcendent Ground of all being—the thing is immemorial and universal. (p. vii)

More recently Ken Wilber (1997) has written extensively about the perennial philosophy.

In my view the perennial philosophy contains the following elements:

1. There is an interconnectedness of reality and a mysterious unity (e.g., Huxley's divine Reality) in the universe.

2. There is an intimate connection between the individual's inner self, or soul, and this mysterious unity.

3. Knowledge of this mysterious unity can be developed through various contemplative practices.

4. Values are derived from seeing and realizing the interconnectedness of reality.

5. This realization can lead to social activity designed to counter injustice and human suffering.

It is important not to approach the perennial philosophy in a reductionistic manner (Ferrer, 2002). The universality of the perennial philosophy must also respect the diversity of spiritual traditions and practices. Ferrer calls for a "more relaxed universalism" that acknowledges the mysterious relationship between the One and Many. It is within this spirit that I attempt to outline in more detail the major principles of the perennial philosophy. Although Ferrer is critical of the term "perennial" philosophy, I think it is possible to have a relaxed universalism using the term "perennial" but bringing a stronger awareness and respect for pluralistic approaches to spirituality and spiritual practices. For this purpose I draw on the following individuals: Gandhi (Hinduism), the Dalai Lama (Buddhism), Emerson (Transcendentalism), and Thomas Merton (Christian Mysticism).

The Interconnected Nature of Reality and the Mysterious Unity of the Universe

The perennial philosophy acknowledges diversity and that the universe is in process; however, underlying the diversity and change is a unity. This unity, however, is not monistic; instead, the emphasis is on the relationships between the whole and the part, or the one and the many. In fact, it is this relationship that is at the heart of the perennial philosophy. Ferrer refers to Martin Buber (1970) and

Mendes-Flohr (1989) and the realm of "the Between" which is the place between objects. This is the mysterious nature of relationship and of the divine unity. Also relationship is not static but dynamic. David Bohm (1980) referred to this as *holomovement* and he stated that "holomovement is undefinable and immeasurable" (p. 151).

For Gandhi (1980), this unity reveals itself in the immediacy of daily life. He also claims that this unity lies behind all religions. He said, "The forms are many, but the informing spirit is one. How can there be room for distinctions of high and low where there is this all-embracing fundamental unity underlying the outward diversity? For that is a fact meeting you at every step in daily life. The final goal of all religions is to realize this essential oneness" (p. 63). Gandhi's position, that this unity is evident in everyday life, reflects the notion that the interconnectedness of reality should not be relegated to remote forms of mysticism.

Interconnectedness and interdependence also lie at the heart of Buddhism. In speaking about concepts, the Dalai Lama (1995) says: "We will find that many of our concepts indicate a very deep, very complex inter-connectedness. For instance, when we speak of ourselves as subjects, we can make sense of that notion only in relation to an object—the idea of a subject makes sense only in relation to an object" (p. 110).

Einstein (1984) spoke of a cosmic religion which involves an awareness of the harmony of nature:

> The individual feels the sublimity and marvelous order which reveal themselves both in nature and in the world of thought. Individual existence impresses him as a sort of prison and he wants to experience the universe as a single significant whole. (p. 102)

The Intimate Connection Between the Individual's Inner Self, or Soul, and the Mysterious Unity

In his journal Emerson (1909–14) stated:

> A man finds out that there is somewhat in him that knows more than he does. Then he comes presently to the curious question, Who's who? which of these two is really me? the one that knows more or the one that knows less: the little fellow or the big fellow. (Vol. 9, p. 190)

Emerson's little fellow is our personal ego which strives to impose its will on the universe. The big fellow which is referred to as the Atman (Hinduism), Kingdom of God within (Christianity) and Buddha nature (Buddhism) realizes the futility of such endeavors and merely seeks to be in tune with the unity. When we are in touch with the "big fellow," we "are not to do, but let do, not to work, but to be worked upon." With the little fellow, we strive and manipulate; with the big fellow, we listen and see and, according to Emerson, are subject to a "vast and sudden enlargement of power" (1909–14). Emerson is referring to the creative power that is similar to Einstein's cosmic religion that inspires the artist and the scientist.

Wisdom or Knowledge of the Mysterious Unity Can Be Developed Through Various Contemplative Practices

A consistent thread in the perennial philosophy is that the rational mind, which focuses on analysis, cannot fully grasp the wholeness of existence. Instead, intuition should be cultivated in order to see more clearly the interrelatedness of reality. Gandhi (1980) refers to intuition as that "still small voice within" that prods him to social action: "There are moments in your life when you must act, even though you cannot carry your best friends with you. The 'still small voice' within you must always be the final arbiter when there is conflict of duty." (p. 62).

Specific approaches have been advocated to cultivate intuition. These methods, which include contemplative practices (e.g., meditation), body work, and loving service, have been developed to help one to "see." Again, this seeing is usually a gradual awakening to the interconnectedness of things.

Emerson, for example, suggested that it was helpful to be quiet and to listen. In this quiet, we can gain access to the "infinitude" within each person. Gandhi (1980) believed that silence was helpful in seeking God. He said, "It [silence] has now become both a physical and spiritual necessity for me. Originally it was taken to relieve the sense of pressure. Then I wanted time for writing. After, however, I had practiced it for some time, I saw the spiritual value of it. It suddenly flashed across my mind that that was the time when I could best hold communion with God. And now I feel as though I was naturally built for silence" (p. 101).

The contemplation of Emerson, however, is different from Gandhi's meditation. In eastern practices meditation tends to be more focused (e.g., repeating a mantra or counting one's breath) than contemplation, which is more unstructured. It is important to realize the diversity of methods used to come in contact with the unity and not assign priority to any one method or practice (Ferrer, 2002).

Values Are Derived From Seeing and Realizing the Interconnectedness of Reality

Values are derived from realizing the fundamental connectedness between individuals; in other words, values are linked to relatedness. Positive values enhance or realize relatedness, and negative values foster separateness and paranoia. Compassion, for example, is a central value in the perennial philosophy. The Dalai Lama consistently refers to the importance of compassion. If we experience interconnectedness and interdependence, a natural sense of compassion for all beings tends to arise. Not seeing ourselves as separate, we feel a basic connection to living beings, both human and non-human. According to the Dalai Lama (1995), "compassion is based on a clear acceptance or recognition that others, like oneself, want happiness and have the right to overcome suffering. On that basis one develops some kind of concern about the welfare of others, irrespective of one's attitude to oneself. That is compassion" (p. 63). He also refers to importance of compassion and loving kindness in all relationships including teaching. At one point he says: "it is my experience that those lessons which we learn from teachers who are not just good, but who also show affection for the student, go deep into our minds" (p. 60). He adds: "compassion for the students' lives or futures, not only for their examinations, makes your work as a teacher much more effective" (p. 72).

Thomas Merton (1959) also wrote about compassion which arises out of a sensitivity to another's inner life. He said: "Compassion and respect enable us to know the solitude of another by finding him in the intimacy of our own interior solitude" (p. 135).

An Awareness of the Mysterious Unity of Existence Leads to Social Action to Counter Injustice and Human Suffering

This last principle is usually not included in descriptions of the perennial philosophy but I believe it arises from the other principles.

If human beings realize they are part of a fundamental unity, then they naturally feel a connectedness and responsibility to others. Most important is the idea that social reform should start from within. According to Emerson (1903–04):

> The origin of all reform is in that mysterious fountain of the moral sentiment in man, which, amidst the natural, ever contains the supernatural for men. That is new and creative. That is alive. That alone can make a man other than he is." (Vol. 1, p. 272)

Emerson's "moral sentiment" is analogous to his "big fellow," which is connected to something bigger than oneself. Although Emerson was not a social activist, he spoke out against slavery and particularly against Daniel Webster's support of the Fugitive Slave Law. He also opposed the exclusion of the Cherokee Indians from Georgia and supported women's rights.

Gandhi, of course, was a social activist who used *ahimsa* (nonviolence) and *satyagraha* (soul force) as vehicles for social change. For Gandhi (1980), religion and politics cannot be compartmentalized:

> I could not be leading a religious life unless I identified myself with the whole of mankind, and that I could not do unless I took part in politics. The whole gamut of man's activities today constitutes an indivisible whole. You cannot divide social, economic, political and purely religious work into watertight compartments. I do not know any religion apart from human activity. It provides a moral basis to all other activities which they would otherwise lack, reducing life to a maze of 'sound and fury signifying nothing.' (p. 63)

Based on his holistic perspective, Gandhi did act to relieve the suffering of his people and to help India become independent of British rule. What is instructive about Gandhi is that his social activity tended to be self-based rather than ego-based. The famous salt march to the sea is a good example of this, as the idea for the march came to him in a dream one night after months of meditation and reflection. Some people (Fischer, 1954) have argued that the salt march was the most important event leading to Indian independence.

Merton (1959) wrote about a "theology of love" which must address injustice in the world. He said this theology "must seek to deal realistically with the evil and injustice in the world, and not merely to compromise with them. . . . Theology does not exist merely to appease the already too untroubled conscience of the powerful and the established" (p. 129).

If the perennial philosophy focuses solely on spiritual practices without reference to the relief of suffering, then there is the danger of narcissism. Ultimately, the perennial philosophy and related practices should lead to an active and dynamic love. This love arises from a deep sense of connection to the earth, all living beings, and the cosmos.

REFERENCES

Bohm, D. (1980). *Wholeness and the implicate order.* London: Routledge & Kegan Paul.

Buber, M. (1970). *I and thou* (W. Kaufman, Trans.). New York: Scribner.

Dalai Lama. (1995). *The power of compassion.* San Francisco: Thorsons.

Einstein, A. (1984). Cosmic religious feeling. In K. Wilber (Ed.), *Quantum Questions* (pp. 101–104). Boulder, CO: Shambhala.

Emerson, R. W. (1903–04). *The complete works: Vol. III* (E. W. Emerson, Ed.). Boston: Houghton Mifflin.

Emerson, R. W. (1909–14). *The journals of Ralph Waldo Emerson: Vol. 9* (E. W. Emerson & W. E. Forbes, Eds.). Boston: Houghton Mifflin.

Emerson, R. W. (1965). *Selected writings* (W. H. Gilman, Ed.). New York: New American Library.

Ferrer, J. N. (2002). *Revisioning transpersonal theory: A participatory vision of human spirituality.* Albany, NY: SUNY Press.

Fischer, L. (1954). *Ghandi: His life and message for the world.* New York: Mentor.

Gandhi, M. (1980). *All men are brothers: Autobiographical reflections.* (K. Kripalani, Ed.). New York: Continuum.

Gordon, K. (2003). The impermanence of being: Towards a psychology of uncertainty. *Journal of Humanistic Psychology, 43*(2), 96–117.

Huxley, A. (1970). *The perennial philosophy.* New York: Harper Colophon.

Mendes-Flohr, P. (1989). *From mysticism to dialogue: Martin Buber's transformation of German social thought.* Detroit, MI: Wayne State University Press.

Merton, T. (1959). *The inner experience.* Unpublished manuscript, fourth draft.

Wilber, K. (1997). *The eye of the spirit: An integral vision for a world gone slightly mad.* Boston: Shambhala.

PART II

Timeless Learning: Processes and Practices

CHAPTER THREE

Letting Go and Becoming Empty

And so it is with man. If he could only pass empty through life, who would be able to injure him?

—Chuang-tzu

Timeless learning involves letting go and emptying ourselves of concepts and models. The mind filled with too many facts, concepts, and models actually gets in the away of learning from a spiritual perspective. Emptying the mind has been central to most spiritual traditions. Angelus Silesius, a Renaissance Christian mystic, explained:

God whose love and joy are everywhere

Can't come to visit

Unless you aren't there.

(cited in Kornfield, 2000, p. 74)

The Buddhist monk, Shunryu Suzuki (1970), stated that we need to have a housecleaning of our minds:

So we say true understanding will come out of emptiness. When you study Buddhism, you have a general house cleaning of your mind. You must take everything out of your room and clean it thoroughly. . . .

One after another you will have thoughts in your mind, but if you want to stop your thinking you can. . . . But as long as you have some fixed idea or are caught by some habitual way of doing things, you cannot appreciate things in their true sense. (p. 112)

Shunryu Suzuki (1970) also used the term *beginner's mind* to describe a mind that is "empty, free of the habits of the expert, ready to accept, to doubt, and open to all the possibilities. It is the kind of mind which can see things as they are" (p. 14).

Thoreau made the same point in a manner more directly related to education when he said: "It is only when we forget our learning that we begin to know. I do not get nearer by a hair's breadth to any natural object so long as I presume that I have an introduction to it from some learned man. To conceive of it with a total apprehension I must for the thousandth time approach it as something totally strange. If you would make acquaintance with the ferns you must forget your botany" (cited in Bickman, 1999, p. 2).

Thoreau is not suggesting giving up the study of botany but advocating the use of mindfulness or presence when we observe an object. The famous Harvard biologist, Louis Agassiz, developed this approach in his teaching. He would give the students a natural object such as a fish to study and ask them to look at it closely and then produce an accurate description of the object before they could proceed with further investigation. This sometimes required hours, or even weeks, of looking at the fish (Menand, 2001, p. 100).

We have paid a price for stressing knowledge over the development of the whole person. Larry Rosenberg (1999) tells the following story about accumulating factual knowledge:

The shortcomings of that kind of knowledge were brought home to me more than twenty years ago, when I was in Korea and studied with a monk named Byok Jo Sunim, one of the most memorable people I've encountered. He almost visibly glowed, radiating the joy that practice brought him. He was extremely loving, had a wonderful sense of humor. He was also completely illiterate. He couldn't sign his name.

While talking with him through an interpreter one day I discovered that he thought the world was flat. I was absolutely astounded and naturally decided to straighten him out. (p. 156)

Rosenberg tried to convince the monk but had no effect with his arguments. Finally the monk said: "Okay. Maybe you Westerners are right. I'm just an illiterate old man. The world is round, and you know that, and I'm too stupid to grasp it. . . . But has knowing that made you any happier? Has it helped you solve your problems in living?" Rosenberg had to agree that much of the knowledge that we accumulate has not helped with the basic issues of living and getting along with one another. The strongest example of this is how Germany had one of the most "educated" populations in the world. Many of these "educated" Germans conducted the extermination of six million Jews and millions of homosexuals. Many others turned a blind eye.

Of course, what the monk and Rosenberg assert is against everything that our current educational system stands for, which occasionally gives lip service to approaches like character education but devotes almost all time and energy to the accumulation of skills and knowledge. But it is important to begin to ask the most fundamental questions about the present system. These questions include what really is important in life and how education can contribute to what is fundamental to living. Of course, knowledge is crucial to making our way in the world but too often we get lost in accumulating knowledge rather than seeing a more basic wisdom. The metaphor of getting lost in the trees (knowledge) rather than seeing the whole forest (wisdom) is appropriate here.

Let's turn now to various approaches to letting go.

PSYCHOSYNTHESIS AND DISIDENTIFICATION

Psychosynthesis is a spiritual psychology developed by Roberto Assagioli (1971). It contains many methods including a process called *disidentification*. This is essentially a letting go of our self-identifications and involves examining our beliefs, desires, opinions, and roles. Piero Ferrucci (1982) has also written about psychosynthesis and suggests that overidentification can lead to the following problems:

A body state tends to become a tension.

A feeling tends to become hangup.

A desire tends to become a compulsive craving.

An opinion tends to become a prejudice.

A role tends to become a mask. (p. 63)

Disidentification involves observing in a nonjudgmental, compassionate manner. Assagioli outlines the basic steps of the process as he suggests repeating the following phrases:

I have a body, but I am not my body.

I have feelings, but I am not my feelings.

I have desires, but I am not my desires.

I have a mind, but I am not my mind.

(cited in Ferrucci, 1982, p. 67)

Assagioli and Ferrucci also introduce the concept of *subpersonality*. They suggest that we may have several subpersonalities such as the Complainer, the Artist, Santa Claus, the Skeptic, the Insecure One, the Clown, "I Told You So," and so on. Disidentification allows us to look at each of these subpersonalities and to choose not to over-identify with them, thus beginning the process of letting go.

David Hunt

One of my colleagues at Ontario Institute for Studies in Education at the University of Toronto, Dave Hunt, has worked many years with of the process of letting go. He begins his classes with exercises that focus on letting go. He refers to Thomas Moore's ideas which suggest that soul work requires "getting out of the way."

Below is one of the exercises that he uses:

I usually begin with a very simple exercise to illustrate two points: (1) you need to let go before you can open up and (2) you can choose to let go. Here's the exercise:

Extend your right arm and make a very tight fist with your right hand . . . take a few moments to experience the tightness and let it represent the unwanted stress you may experience . . . send a signal down your arm to gradually release the tension and feel your fingers loosening . . . when your hand is relaxed turn over your hand and look at the open palm. After some reflection, the exercise is repeated with both hands. (Hunt, 1999, pp. 44–45)

Hunt then describes the experience of one of his students:

[One hand] I make a fist. The tension extends from my hand to my arm, shoulder, chest, and eventually to all parts of my body . . . tension throbbing, hurting. Just when I think I can't stand the tension much longer, I will my fist to relax, and relaxation radiates gradually all through my body. The release is beautiful . . . my fingers tingle, my senses are heightened. When I turn my hand over my open hand, soft, welcoming, unprotected, open I am wonderfully surprised at the realization that letting go is a choice I made.

[Two hands] Again I am elated at the realization that I can choose to let go—that letting go is the prerequisite to opening up. The sight of my open hands has deep spiritual significance for me—I am open to the transcendent. My hands are peaceful, welcoming, open to surprise. . . . When I clasp my hands together, I feel warmth and gentleness. When I am gentle with myself, I feel connected. (p. 45)

Finally, Hunt believes that one of aspects that many people need to let go of is what he calls the inner critic. He cites Stephen Nachmanovitch (1990) in this regard:

It is our automatic internalization of parental and other judging voices that throw doubt on whether we are good enough, smart enough, the right size or shape, and also of the wishful voices that indicate who we should be and what we should like to have. Both hope and fear are functions of the judging specter. (p. 38)

Hunt suggests that he has found that his students mention three strategies that are very helpful in dealing with the inner critic: nature, friends, and humor. For example, one person said that going for walk in nature helped to clear the mind. Humor, and the ability to laugh at oneself, is also very helpful in loosening the power of the inner critic.

KRISHNAMURTI

This emptying of the mind applied not only to observation of the external world but to the inner world as well. Krishnamurti felt that one of the main goals of education should be an awareness of our conditioning so that we can begin to let go of its effects. He (1953) said that:

> It is the function of the educator to examine deeply his own thoughts and feelings and to *put aside* those values which have given him security and comfort, for only then can he help his students to be self-aware and to understand their own urges and fears. (p. 38, italics mine)

Krishnamurti was not an advocate of specific methods either in spiritual practice or in teaching but it is clear that he is suggesting that teachers and students look at their own conditioning. This can begin with a still or contemplative mind. In a talk with students Krishnamurti (1974) describes the process of meditation as way to still the mind and let go of conditioning:

> Meditation is something extraordinary, if you know how to do it. I am going to talk a little about it.
> First of all, sit very quietly; do not force yourself to sit quietly, but sit or lie down quietly without force of any kind. . . . Then watch your thinking. Watch what you are thinking about. You find you are thinking about your shoes, your saris, what you are going to say, the bird outside to which you listen; follow such thoughts and enquire why each thought arises. Do not try to change your thinking. See why certain thoughts arise in your mind so that you begin to understand the meaning of every thought and every feeling without any enforcement. And when a thought arises, do not condemn it, do not say it is right, it is wrong, it is good, it is bad. Just watch it so that you begin to

have perception, a consciousness which is active in seeing every kind of thought, every kind of feeling. . . . The mind is completely awake. (p. 59)

What kind of condition is Krishnamurti referring to? Primarily it is psychological conditioning where we have had values instilled by political, religious, and educational institutions. Krishnamurti's work in education is described in more detail in Chapter 8.

THE *BHAGAVAD GITA* AND NONATTACHMENT

The *Gita* is one of the central texts of Hinduism; Gandhi read it everyday of his adult life. One of the central ideas and practices is not being attached to the results of our actions. This is another way of letting go. In the *Gita* Krishna states: "The man whose consciousness is unified abandons all attachment to the results of actions and attains supreme peace. But the man whose desires are fragmented, and who is selfishly attached to the results of his work, is bound in all he does" (Easwaran, 1975, p. 310).

If we are attached to the results of our actions then we cannot be fully present. We already have an agenda. Certainly there are degrees of attachment and if the attachment is strong it can control most of our behavior. Desires for money, power, and fame are among the most familiar attachments which can consume our lives.

Meditation is a process which lets us witness our attachments. We can begin to see clearly what we cling to. These are the thoughts and agendas that recur constantly in our minds. Just witnessing these thoughts and attachments can be the beginning of freedom. Of course, this inner freedom does not come instantly; in fact, it may take most of our lives to realize.

Hinduism is not the only faith to advocate nonattachment. St. John of the Cross wrote: "The soul that is attached to anything, however much good there may be in it, will not arrive at the liberty of divine union" (cited in Huxley, 1970, p. 105). Chuang-tzu, the Taoist master, stated: "And so it is with man. If he could only pass empty through life, who would be able to injure him?" (Huxley, p. 106). Finally there is a Sufi aphorism which says: "When the heart weeps for what it has lost, the spirit laughs for what is has found" (Huxley, p. 106).

Spiritual Knowing

From a spiritual perspective, when we start to empty and let go of our attachments, a deeper knowing or wisdom can arise. In the silence and emptiness we begin to see things more clearly. We can begin to discern which kinds of knowledge are important and which are not. Aldous Huxley suggests that by letting go we can access spiritual knowledge which can encourage further release. However, if we do not make the effort to let go, we can be seduced into an empty intellectualism. Huxley (1970) quotes the *Theologica Germanica* to make his point: "Some men love knowledge and discernment as the best and most excellent of all things. Behold, then knowledge and discernment come to be loved more than that which is discerned" (p. 111).

Attachment to knowledge and learning leads easily to a false sense of security and even superiority. As the individual accumulates more knowledge it is easy to feel somehow better than or superior to those who know less. Christopher Titmus (1993), a meditation teacher, comments: "Goal-focused learning ignores the potential to develop in a noncompetitive, non-goal-oriented way. . . . Superiority, arrogance and pride may be the fruits of 'success' while inferiority, disappointment and envy may be the fruits of 'failure'" (p. 111).

We have forgotten the insights of John Holt (1964) and others about how our educational system instills in many children a deep sense of failure. In *How Children Fail* Holt argued that schools teach children how to conform rather than to think for themselves. Writers such as Paul Goodman (1960) and Jonathan Kozol (1967) made similar arguments.

Spiritual wisdom can help us develop a different approach to learning that is truly life affirming. I believe that such an approach would help develop human beings who are whole and happy. I close this chapter with the words of Achaan Chah (1985) the Buddhist monk who said this about letting go:

Just Let Go

Do everything with a mind that lets go. Do not expect any praise or reward. If you let go a little, you will have a little peace. If you let go a lot, you will have a lot of peace. If you let go completely, you will know complete peace and freedom. Your struggles with the world will have come to an end. (p. 73)

REFERENCES

Assagioli, R. (1971). *Psychosynthesis.* New York: Viking Press.

Bickman, M. (1999). *Uncommon learning: Henry David Thoreau on education.* Boston: Houghton Mifflin.

Chah, A. (1985). *A still forest pool.* (J. Kornfield & P. Breiter, Eds.). Wheaton, IL: Theosophical.

Easwaran, E. (1975). *The end of sorrow: The Bhagavad Gita for daily living: Vol. 1.* Petaluma, CA: Nilgiri.

Ferrucci, P. (1982). *What we may be: Techniques for psychological and spiritual growth.* Los Angeles: Jeremy P. Tarcher.

Goodman, P. (1960). *Growing up absurd.* New York: Vintage.

Holt, J. (1964). *How children fail.* New York: Pitman.

Hunt, D. (1999). Letting go. *Orbit, 30*(2), 44–47.

Huxley, A. (1970). *The perennial philosophy.* New York: Harper Colophon.

Kozol, J. (1967). *Death at an early age.* Boston: Houghton Mifflin.

Krishnamurti, J. (1953). *Education and the significance of life.* New York: Harper & Row.

Krishnamurti, J. (1974). *Krishnamurti on education.* New York: Harper & Row.

Kornfield, J. (2000). *After the ecstasy, the laundry: How the heart grows wise on the spiritual path.* New York: Bantam.

Menand, L. (2001). *The metaphysical club: A story of ideas in America.* New York: Farrar, Straus, and Giroux.

Nachmanovitch, S. (1990). *Free play.* New York: Jeremy P. Tarcher/Putnam.

Rosenberg, L. (1999). Beyond letting go: Moving into deep silence. In S. Salzberg (Ed.), *Voices of insight* (pp. 154–167). Boston: Shambhala.

Suzuki, S. (1970). *Zen mind, beginner's mind: Informal talks on Zen meditation and practice.* New York: Weatherhill.

Titmus, C. (1993). *The profound and the profane: An inquiry into spiritual awakening.* Devon, UK: Insight Books.

CHAPTER FOUR

Attention and Meditation

We carry with us the wonders we seek without us.

—Sir Thomas Browne

Attention! Attention! Attention!

A student of Zen purchased a spiritual text. Bringing it to the monastery, the student asked if the teacher would write some words of inspiration in it.

"Certainly," replied the teacher, who wrote for a second then handed the book back. There the student found only a single word: " Attention!"

"Will you not write more?" pleaded the disappointed student, again offering the book to the teacher.

"All right," said the teacher, who this time wrote for several seconds. Inside the book the student now found three words: "Attention! Attention! Attention!"

(cited in Walsh, 1999, p. 150)

Attention is fundamental to spiritual practice. There can be little learning with a wandering mind. When one begins a practice such as meditation, one immediately becomes aware of how difficult it is to hold the attention on a single object such as the breath or a mantra. The thoughts intrude immediately.

The problem of paying attention is not limited to meditation. In schools teachers are familiar with children with attention deficit disorder (ADD). These children move quickly from one thing to another without completing the previous task. They have difficulty not only in academic work but in relationships.

It can be argued that these children simply represent a more extreme version of an aspect of our culture—the short attention span. Videos, television shows, and much of our entertainment are based on the assumption of limited attention. We often feel the need to do two or three things at once because we become bored if we are simply doing one thing. If we become bored watching one show, we can use the remote to move through all the channels which can now number in the hundreds. The restless mind is constantly seeking to be entertained.

Maintaining attention then in our society is a challenge. The spiritual traditions can help us, as attention is central to spiritual growth and development. There are various forms of attention. Theravadan Buddhists refer to *bare attention.* This type of attention is simply being present to what is happening. It is does not embellish experience or make a story of it.

Another form of attention is *compassionate attention.* It arises from a sense of connection with the object of attention. It is an active, not a passive, form of attention. Compassionate attention is close to what Ken McLeod (2001) calls *pristine awareness* (p. 27). Here attention is not separate from experience. McLeod gives an example of pristine awareness when he says: "In a conversation with a close friend about a tragedy, time stops, yet the conversation continues. Although you may not remember what was said, the experience of presence remains with you" (p. 27). McLeod identifies an important aspect of attention that relates to the main theme of this book when he states that "time stops"; deep attention then is timeless.

McLeod also identifies three stages to develop attention. The first stage is *formal practice,* which includes meditation practice which will be discussed in more detail in this chapter. Meditation practice almost always starts with focusing the attention on some object such as the breath, a sound, or an image. The next stage is extending the attention into daily life. This usually starts with simple activities such as walking, washing the dishes, and folding the laundry. This application of attention to daily life is also called *mindfulness.* The third and final stage that McLeod describes is *living in attention.* Here attention is no longer just a practice but an ongoing reality in our everyday lives. It is something that then can arise naturally in our life and work and is often the outcome of many years of meditation and mindfulness practice.

MEDITATION

In the West we tend to associate meditation with gurus and mysticism, which is unfortunate. Meditation is a simple practice that focuses on the development of attention. There is ample evidence to support the value of meditative practice which is discussed in the last chapter.

FORMS OF MEDITATION

When one is just beginning meditation practice it is helpful to pick a method one feels comfortable with. It is possible to categorize approaches to meditation according to four different types: *intellectual, emotional, physical,* and *action-service.*

Intellectual Meditation

Intellectual approaches to meditation focus on awareness and discrimination. Meditation is seen as a form of inquiry to the mind-body process. This is not inquiry as we traditionally use in the West, which is viewed as problem solving; instead, meditative inquiry is a deeper form of inquiry into the basic processes of life. Insight, or *vipassana* meditation, which comes from the teachings of the Buddha, can be looked at in this light. Krishnamurti also practiced a form of meditative inquiry. He would take a question and then explore it completely. For example, Krishnamurti (1963) was asked the question, "How is one to be intelligent?"

> What is implied in this question? You want a method by which to be intelligent—which implies that you know what intelligence is. When you want to go some place, you already know your destination and you only have to ask the way. Similarly, you think you know what intelligence is, and you want a method by which you can be intelligent. Intelligence is the very questioning

of the method. Fear destroys intelligence does it not? Fear prevents you from examining, questioning, inquiring; it prevents you from finding out what is true. Probably you will be intelligent when there is no fear. So you have to inquire into the whole question of fear, and be free of fear; and then there is the possibility of you being intelligent. But if you say, "How am I to be intelligent?" You are merely cultivating a method and so you become stupid. (p. 40)

Emotional Meditation

These forms of meditation connect with the heart. Mantra meditation which involves repeating a phrase or word over and over can be emotionally oriented. One of the classic Christian mantras is the Jesus prayer: "Lord Jesus, Son of God, have mercy on me, a sinner." *The Way of the Pilgrim,* a classic in the spiritual literature, describes how a Russian monk, traveling in Russia, constantly repeated the Jesus prayer and how this process transformed him and those that he came in contact with. If he was hungry or cold he would recite the prayer and found that he could overcome many difficulties that he encountered. In the Hindu religion the devotee recites the name of God, *Ram,* over and over again. Gandhi practiced this mantra most of his life.

Physical Meditation

Physical meditation involves various forms of movement. Hatha yoga, tai chi, akido, and the martial arts are movement meditations. The practitioner is deeply attentive to the physical movement. This type of meditation can appeal to people who prefer to move rather than sit. Below is an example of a physical approach to meditation:

There is the Hasidic tale of the great Rabbi who was coming to visit a small town in Russia. It was a very great event for the Jews in the town and each thought long and hard about what questions they would ask the wise man. When he finally arrived, all were gathered in the largest available room and each was deeply concerned with the questions they had for him. The Rabbi came into the room and felt the great tension in it. For a time he said nothing and then began to hum softly a Hasidic tune. Presently all there were humming with him. He then began to sing the song and soon all were singing with him. Then he began to dance and soon all present were deeply involved in the dance, all fully committed to it, all just dancing and nothing else. In this way, each one became whole with himself, each healed the splits within himself which kept him from understanding. After the dance went on for a time, the Rabbi gradually slowed it to a stop, looked at the group, and said, "I trust that I have answered all your questions." (LeShan, 1974, pp. 50–51)

Action Meditation

Action meditation is service oriented. One works in the world with the idea that each act is an offering to the divine. The work of Mother Teresa can be seen in this light. The action is not viewed as a way of improving or the changing the world. Instead the action is performed in a way that lets us deepen our relationship with the Mystery. The world is seen as a vast schoolroom where we are presented with what we need to learn at each moment in our lives.

In Hinduism this is called *karma yoga*. Huston Smith (1986) describes the basic approach:

The world is the soul's gymnasium, its school, its training field. What we do is important, but ultimately it is important for the discipline it offers our individual spirits; we delude ourselves if we expect it to change the world in any fundamental way. Our work in this world is like bowling in an uphill alley; it can develop nice muscles, but we should not think that by our throws the balls are transported to the other end in any permanent way. They all roll back eventually to confront our children if we happen to have moved along. The world can develop character and teach men to look beyond it—for these it is admirably suited—but it can be converted into a paradise in which man is fully at home. "Said Jesus, blessed be his name, this world is a bridge; pass over it, but build no house upon it." (p. 108)

We turn now to the various types of meditation.

MEDITATION PRACTICES

Insight

Insight, or *vipassana,* meditation focuses on being aware of what happens in each moment. This meditation usually starts with an awareness of the flow of the breath. One simply follows either the breath coming in and out of the nostrils or the rising and falling of the abdomen. The eyes are usually closed and we can label the flow of the breath with "in and out" for the nostrils or "rising and falling" for the abdomen. Insight meditation, however, does not stay with the breath as the sole focus. Although it is the anchor to which we can always return, the awareness gradually moves to other phenomena. For example, the awareness can also focus on the sensations that may arise in the body. If our knee starts to hurt, or our arm itches, the attention can shift to these sensations. The mind simply notices these sensations as they arise and stays focused on them and then notices them passing away. The term *insight* is based on watching this arising and passing away of phenomena.

Another area that we can focus on are feelings which can arise during meditation. For example, if we have had an argument with our spouse, we can be filled with feelings of anger. These feelings can sometimes be very powerful so that they take over and we lose our basic awareness of what is happening. Here we can come back to the breath to gain our balance and then return to an awareness of the anger. Insight can also come from witnessing that we are not the anger which arises and then passes away. Yes, there are these feelings, but because they are impermanent we gain understanding that we don't have to identify or to become the feeling.

Another area of focus is our thoughts. Our mind is filled with thoughts and again we can be taken over by them. For example, thoughts relating to our work can be quite strong, and during our meditation we simply try to stay aware of these thoughts. One technique for watching our thoughts is to see them as clouds floating by. Another technique is to label the thoughts. At a general level we can label all thoughts as "thinking," or we can be more specific and label the nature of the thoughts. For example, we can use labels like "planning," "remembering," or "imagining." Shunryu Suzuki gives some helpful advice when observing our thoughts. They relate to the metaphor of "big mind" discussed earlier:

When you are practicing Zazen meditation do not try to stop your thinking. Let it stop by itself. If something comes into your mind, let it come in and let it go out. It will not stay long. When you try to stop your thinking, it means you are bothered by it. Do not be bothered by anything. It appears that the something comes from outside your mind, but actually it is only the waves of your mind and if you are not bothered by the waves, gradually they will become calmer and calmer . . . If you leave your mind as it is, it will become calm. This mind is called big mind. (cited in Goldstein, 1976, p. 28)

Suzuki also advises that we can welcome the thoughts but we should not serve them tea. In meditation we are not trying to clear the mind or create some model of what the mind should be. Instead we are simply being present to what is happening.

Another focus for the insight process is sound. If any sound arises, then our attention turns to the sound. If a car passes outside or someone turns on the television in the next apartment, we notice the sound and then return to the breathing again as our anchor.

Eventually with the insight meditation our attention shifts to whatever is predominant in the moment. For example, if my back is sore, my attention shifts to the soreness. If my thoughts start to react to the pain, I notice these thoughts. If any related feelings arise, I notice these feelings. If my mind becomes too unsettled by all this, I simply return to the breath. Gradually, however, this meditation allows me to live in the present moment. It allows our natural awareness to arise so that we are not encumbered by our thoughts and feelings. We experience more fully each moment rather than living in the past or projecting ourselves into the future. We gradually learn that all we really have to experience is what is happening right now.

One of the best books on insight meditation is Joseph Goldstein's *The Experience of Insight: A Natural Unfolding*. In this book, Goldstein (1976) says:

Just let things happen as they do. Let all images and thoughts and sensations rise and pass away without being bothered, without reacting, without judging, without clinging, without identifying with them. Become one with the big mind, observing carefully, microscopically, all the waves coming and going. This attitude will quickly bring about a state of balance and calm. Don't let the mind get out of focus. Keep the mind sharply aware, moment to moment of what is happening, whether the in-out breath sensations, or thoughts. In each instant be focused on the object with a balanced and relaxed mind. (p. 28)

Body Scan

The body is also an excellent anchor for meditation practice and helps us move away from being just in our heads. Also called *body sweeping,* this technique has been taught by Jon Kabat-Zinn and S. N. Goenka. Kabat-Zinn describes his approach in *Full Catastrophe Living* (1990) while Goenka's elaboration on the body scan is described in Hart (1987). The technique starts either at the top of the head or the toes and gradually moves through the entire body. Below are some basic instructions:

Begin by focusing the attention at the top of the head. Note any sensations there. Do you notice any pulsing, itching, or tightness or is there not any particular sensation that arises? Now move the attention to the back of the head. Again be aware of any sensations there. If there is a sensation focus on that for the moment. Now shift the attention to the left side of the head and then the right side. What sensations do you notice there? Now focus on the face. Be aware of any sensations that arise around the eyes, nose of mouth.

Now focus on the front of the neck and then gradually move to the sides of the neck and finally the back of the neck. Now gradually move the attention down the back. First, focus on the shoulders and then gradually move to the top of the back. Move slowly down the back noticing any sensation. Tension can be held in the shoulders and the back so move slowly through this area of the body noting any tightness or pain. If there is any pain, try not to react to the pain but just notice it in a non-judgmental manner. Soften the attention where is there is pain or tightness.

Shift the awareness now to the arms. Move the attention down the one arm till you reach the hands and the fingers. Again note any sensation or lack thereof. Now move the awareness to the other arm moving the attention down from the shoulder to the hands and fingers.

Focus the attention on the right pelvis area. Now slowly move the awareness down the leg. Focus on the thigh, then the knee. Next scan the lower leg and finally the feet and toes. Shift the attention to the left pelvis area and then move down the leg to the foot and toes noting and sensation that arises. Rest the attention on the feet and toes for a moment.

Now move the awareness back up the body starting with toes and feet and moving through each part again.

After moving through body slowly, you can follow with body scans that are faster as you sweep up and down. The body scan can take as long 45 minutes.

Mantra

Mantra or *mantram* is simply using a word, or phrase, as the anchor of awareness. It is repeated over and over in silent sitting meditation or as we do our daily activities. The word *mantra* comes from the roots *man,* "the mind," and *tri,* "to cross." Easwaran (1977) states that "the mantra is that which enables us to cross the sea of the mind" (p. 43).

Mantra exists in almost all religions. As mentioned earlier, the Jesus prayer is a Christian mantra. *Hail Mary* used in Catholicism is another Christian mantra.

I have already mentioned the mantra *Ram* which Gandhi repeated throughout his life and was on his lips when he died. Another Hindu mantra using Ram is *Om sri Ram jai Ram jai jai Ram.* This mantra simply means "May joy prevail" (Easwaran, 1977 p. 58).

One the most famous mantras in Buddhism is *Om mani padme hum* which refers to the "jewel in the lotus of the heart" (Easwaran, 1977, p. 60). Here the lotus flower is used as a metaphor for purity of heart which can be realized more fully by repeating this mantra.

In Judaism the phrase, *Barukh, attah Adonai,* means "Blessed art thou, oh Lord" (Easwaran, 1977, p. 60). By repeating this phrase the devotee becomes more deeply connected to God.

In the Muslim faith the mantra *Bismillah ir-Rahman ir-Rahim* means "in the name of Allah, the merciful, the compassionate" (Easwaran, 1977, p. 61). According to Easwaran, "Orthodox Muslims say the mantram before they speak, as a reminder that everything we say and everything we do should be in accord with the will of God, in accord with the indivisible unity of life" (p. 61).

Once you have selected a mantra that seems to resonate with you, stick with it. Do not shift mantras during meditation practice. It is also wise not to repeat your mantra to individuals who are not sympathetic to meditation practice. The mantra should not necessarily be a secret; it is just that you want to be able to approach meditation practice with a positive frame of mind.

Having chosen a mantra, you can begin practice. It is best to begin with your eyes open and to repeat the mantra out loud. Once you have a sense of the sound and the rhythm, you can begin to repeat it silently to yourself with your eyes closed or half open. As you repeat the mantra, get the feeling that the mantra is autonomous; that is, it is repeating itself. You are not doing the mantra, but it is going on within you:

> That is all there is to meditating—just sitting peacefully, hearing the mantra in your mind, allowing it to change any way it wants— to get louder or softer—to disappear or return—to stretch out or speed up . . . Meditation is like drifting on a stream in a boat without oars—because you need no oars—you are not going anywhere. (Carrington, 1977, p. 80)

It is also possible to repeat your mantra during the day. For example, the mantra can be repeated while riding the bus or subway. At work, if you begin to feel tense, you can work with the mantra to deal with the tension. Another time that the mantra can be used is when you are walking, as the mantra can provide a silent rhythm to your walk. Other opportunities for mantra include times when you are sick or bored. Occasionally we are presented with long stretches of time when there is nothing to do. Instead of turning on the TV as relief from our boredom we can practice mantra. Another good time for mantra is when you lie awake at night. Instead of letting the random thoughts take over which can often contribute to your restlessness at night, try repeating a mantra. The silent rhythm will focus your mind and may help you return to sleep.

There are times when it is not appropriate to do mantra. For example, if you are doing any job or task which requires your full attention such as driving or listening to music the mantra will be an interference.

Eknath Easwaran (1977) has written a beautiful book on the mantra. He says:

Once the mantram has become an integral part of our consciousness, all mantrams are the same. Whatever Holy Name we use, at this stage it is the perfect embodiment of the Lord of Love.

The Holy Name reverberating in the depths of consciousness transfigures our entire vision of life. Just as the mantram transforms negative forces in consciousness into constructive power, so it now transforms all our perceptions of the everyday world into unbroken awareness of the unity of life. (pp. 246–247)

Of course it is possible to a repeat a mantra that is not connected to a particular religious tradition. For example, the relaxation response asks the person to repeat the number one (Benson, 1976). Sometimes the focus is on the sound of the mantra rather than any meaning. Again, you should be clear in your intention, whether you are doing the mantra just for relaxation or whether there is a religious or spiritual focus.

Visualization

Imagery can be a source of inner growth. An image in our mind can have powerful effects; for example, if I am afraid of public speaking just the image of seeing myself in front of an audience can make my heart beat faster. Guided imagery, or visualization, attempts to elicit images that can foster positive growth and awareness.

Visualization can bring about specific physiological changes. Studies have shown that when an individual imagines himself or herself running, small contractions take place in the muscles associated with running.

We also know that emotional changes can take place through visualization. For example, if we fear flying in an airplane the image of this event can trigger fear and accompanying physiological changes. Similarly, a relaxing image, such as walking in a meadow, can lead to a lower heart rate, lower blood pressure, and relaxed muscles. Studies have been conducted in a number of areas and Murphy (1992) claims that these "studies have shown that imagery practice can facilitate relief from various afflictions, among them depression, anxiety, insomnia, obesity, sexual problems, chronic pain, phobias, psychosomatic illnesses, cancer, and other diseases" (p. 372).

A simple visualization exercise to begin with is one in which you visualize an object, such as an orange:

> Set an orange about two or three feet in front of you. Place the orange so that there are no other objects around it to distract your attention . . . Relax and breathe deeply . . . Now study the orange, notice its shape, color, and any unusual markings, etc. . . . Now close your eyes . . . See the image of the orange, for example, the shape, color and any markings . . . Now open your eyes and look at the orange. Compare it with the image you saw. Notice any differences. Now close your eyes and repeat the exercise. (Miller, 1993, p. 67)

If you have difficulty with this exercise, or with any other, you can come back to it at another time. You may find that images come easier the next time. The following guided imagery is more spiritually oriented:

> Relax. Close your eyes . . . You are in a meadow . . . The sky is blue and you see a hill in the distance . . . What does the hill look like as you approach it? . . . Is the hill large or small? . . . Is it rough and hard to climb or is its surface smooth and easy to scale? . . . You see a path going up the hill and you follow it . . . Is the path wide or narrow? . . . What is the ground like around you as you begin to walk up the path? . . . Is there grass or are there lots of rocks? . . . As you walk up this hill notice the view . . . Stop and look around . . . How far can you see? . . . Now you begin to resume your walk. Smell the fresh air as you walk up the path. You feel invigorated and refreshed as you walk up the hill . . .
>
> You begin to approach the top of the hill and there you see a temple . . . As you approach the temple what does it look like? . . . Notice the form of the building as you approach it. As you approach the temple you feel peaceful and calm . . . You walk to the door of the temple and take your shoes off . . . There is an opening at the top of the temple roof and sunlight is streaming through . . . You walk to the light and stand under it and feel its radiance and warmth . . . Let it permeate and rejuvenate your whole being . . . You are now ready to go to the inner sanctuary . . . There is a symbol or an image in the center of the

room . . . This symbol represents to you an educational ideal. Reflect on this symbol and its meaning for you . . . (Two or three minute pause) . . . Leave the temple and walk slowly down the hill . . . Now you are reaching the bottom of the hill. Take the energy you have received from this journey and use it as you return to your daily life. (Miller, 1993, p. 69)

This guided imagery exercise contains a symbol that each person will imagine and interpret in his or her own way. Symbols are integral to the visualization process. Some common symbols found in fantasies and their possible meanings include:

Water: receptivity, passivity, calm

Ascent: growth, inward journey

Cross: tree of life, spiritual connectedness

Hill or Mountain: aims or ambitions

Light: creativity, unity, spiritual source

Sun: life force, healing spiritual wholeness

(Samuels & Samuels, 1975, p. 97)

A symbol can have many meanings and we should not get too involved in interpreting them. However, if a symbol is persistent you may want to work with it in meditation or other visualizations in order to see its meaning. One of the best books on visualization *is Seeing With the Mind's Eye* by Samuels and Samuels (1975). This book contains a number of visualizations that can be applied to being more creative, dealing with illness, or simply tapping into our spiritual natures.

If we feel a connection to a particular spiritual teacher, we can visualize the presence of that person. We can imagine the energy, love, and compassion flowing from that person into our own hearts. Visualizing the presence of another person is called *kything*. Savary and Berne (1988) define kything as a conscious act of spiritual presence. One example of kything that they cite is from Viktor Frankl's book *Man's Search for Meaning* (1992). One of the ways that Frankl survived in the concentration camp was to imagine the presence of his wife:

As my friend and I stumbled on for miles, slipping on icy spots, supporting each other time and time again, dragging one another up and onward, nothing was said but we both knew; each of us was thinking of his wife. Occasionally I looked at the sky, where the stars were fading and the pink light of the morning was beginning to spread behind a dark bank of clouds. But my mind clung to my wife's image, imagining it with an uncanny acuteness. I heard her answering me, saw her smile, her frank and encouraging look. Real or not, her look was then more luminous than the sun which was beginning to rise. (p. 68)

Frankl's experience demonstrates the power of visualization as it helped him survive the terrible ordeal of the concentration camp. Savary and Berne talk about three modes of presence—physical, psychological, and spiritual. Physical presence is simply being together in the same physical space, while psychological presence involves mind-to-mind communication. Kything at the spiritual level can be described as soul-to-soul encounters that lead to communion.

Movement Meditation

Movement meditations can range from simple walking meditation to yoga to tai chi. Here I briefly describe walking meditation. This meditation is often done in retreats in conjunction with sitting meditation (e.g., insight meditation). For example, the retreat participants alternate between 45 minutes of sitting meditation and 45 minutes of walking meditation.

Start with your eyes looking down a few feet ahead of you.

Stand for a few moments just being aware of your body standing. Let the arms rest at the side. Now focus on your feet. Feel them supporting you and resting on the ground. The attention in this meditation is on the foot as it touches the ground and moves. The foot, then, is the anchor in this exercise. The movement is slow as you lift the foot and gradually place it on the ground.

Just walk a short distance forward (e.g., 10 or 15 yards) and then turn around. As you turn just stop for a moment before you resume your walking.

It is also possible to label the movements so as you lift the foot you might say to yourself "lifting," then "moving" as you move it, and "touching" as it touches the ground again. However, the important thing is to keep the attention focused on the feet and the movements.

At the end of the meditation you can just stand for a few moments being aware of your entire body.

GETTING STARTED

If you have never meditated before, you may want to try the different methods for a while until you find the one you are most comfortable with. Again the approach will probably be congruent with your orientation—intellectual, emotional, physical, or action-service. Once you have settled on an approach stick with it. If you keep changing, your practice will never deepen.

To begin stationary meditation practice, sit comfortably with your head, neck, and chest in a straight line. You can sit in a chair or cross-legged on a cushion or bench. Most important, you should be in a position where you won't be shifting around a lot during the meditation. It is probably best to meditate at least one hour after eating. The times that seem to be most popular for meditation are early in the morning upon arising, before dinner, or late in the evening. You should choose a place free of distractions. If you have a room for meditation, fine; if not, then a corner of a bedroom can also be arranged so that it is conducive to meditation. Once settled on a time and place, others in the household should be made aware that you are not to be disturbed unless there is something urgent. However, you should not be unreasonable about your practice. For example, if there are young children in the household you should probably not choose to meditate right before dinner, as this usually is a busy time around the household and meditation practice could interfere with the needs of the family. Meditation should be done so that family life patterns are not drastically disturbed.

A period of 20 minutes is appropriate to begin meditation practice. As you commit yourself to a particular method, then you can lengthen the period to 30 or 40 minutes. During meditation you can look at your watch to check the time. Timers are also available, but it is perfectly alright to check a watch or clock during the meditation period. At the end remain seated for a minute or two, thus allowing a space between the meditation and the resumption of daily activities.

MEDITATION WITH CHILDREN

Although there are challenges to using meditation in public school classrooms, more and more people are beginning to the make the case for meditation in the schools. Iris Murdoch (1992), the renowned English novelist and philosopher, wrote:

> The damage done to inner life, to aloneness and quietness, through the imposition of banal or pornographic or violent images by television, is a considerable wound. *Teach meditation in schools.* [my italics] Some understanding of, and taste for exercises in detachment and quietness, the sense of another level, and another place, a larger space, might thus be acquired for life. Simply sitting quietly and calmly can be doing something good; subduing unkind or frenzied thoughts certainly is. Morality as the ability or attempt to be good, rests upon deep areas of sensibility and creative imagination, upon removal from one state of mind to another, upon shift of attachments, upon love and respect for the contingent details of the world. (p. 337)

Ms. Murdoch, who certainly was not part of the New Age movement, makes a very strong case for exploring meditation in schools.

In many ways very young children already meditate with their focus on the here and now.

> As children, the play of the sun on rippling water brought us before God's throne. Did you ever see an infant gaze at a light bulb or the moon? Spiritual techniques are discovered naturally by infants and little children: holding their breath, staring unblinking, standing on their heads, imitating animals, turning in circles, sitting unmoving; and repeating phrases over and over until all else ceases to exist. (Ram Dass, 1978, pp. 62–63)

Older children and adolescents, I believe, could benefit from exposure to meditation in schools. Gina Levete (1995), who is associated with the Interlink Trust in England, has been working extensively in the area of meditation in the schools. She cites statements by 14- and 15-year-old children that indicate the need for the development of the inner life.

I do lots of things but inside I feel alone.

I hate doing nothing.

I go to lots of parties but sometimes I think 'what's it all about?'

I always have the radio on for background noise.

Walking is boring unless there is something at the end of it. (p. 1)

Levete argues that meditation could be used in schools if it is presented within a nonreligious framework. She cites Jon Kabat-Zinn (1990) and Clive Erriker (Erriker & Erriker, 2001) as people who have suggested that meditation can be practiced without reference to a specific religious tradition. Kabat-Zinn's techniques are connected to Buddhism, but in his work with people who have chronic pain, he has found the meditation techniques can be adapted without specific reference to religious or spiritual traditions. Kabat-Zinn's work has become well known through his books (1990) and his appearance on the Bill Moyers program, *Healing and the Mind.* During this eight-week program, individuals learn to practice basic breath meditation and mindfulness in a nondogmatic atmosphere. The same principles can be applied within an educational institution.

Levete (1995) suggests that meditation can be used in the elementary school with young children. To support her case she quotes the following individuals (p. 12):

Younger children naturally accept meditation because they don't come with so much baggage. By sixteen they tend to analyze and question the practice.

—Paul Moss, St. James Independent School

I am constantly surprised at the capacity of young boys to sit still. Meditation is, I am sure, of enormous educational as well as spiritual benefit.

—David Lindsay, school chaplain,
Haberdashers Askes School

In this latter school, meditation was introduced as a result of the visit of a Franciscan friar in 1986. Ever since, the school has offered a 15-minute lunchtime meditation for those who want to participate. Numbers at this voluntary session range from 6 to 36 students. Meditation is also introduced to students in a class on Buddhism.

Levete (1995) also cites a teacher at a London primary school who stated that when meditation was introduced to 7- to 8-year-old students, she found that "by the fourth week children were noticeably quieter and more able to concentrate on meditating" (p. 12). Levete visited several schools in England where meditation was being used and came to the following conclusion, "After visiting a number of state and independent schools the overall impression is, that, provided students are presented with clear guidance, meditation for them is almost instinctive" (p. 13).

In general Levete found the following methods being used:

Following the breath

Connecting to the body (e.g., body scan)

Walking meditation

Mantra

Visualization

Observing the mind

Meditation in the school is probably best integrated with other activities. For example, meditation can be done as a centering activity before a stressful activity like taking a test. Similarly, it can also be utilized in conjunction with activities like physical education or drama. Whether the issue is going to bat in baseball or performing one's dramatic role, centering allows students to collect themselves.

One activity that can also be used to help students relax is progressive muscle relaxation. Here, the student is guided to relax muscles throughout the body, starting with the feet. The exercise involves first tensing, holding the tension, and then relaxing the muscles.

The teacher instructs the student approximately as follows:

Begin by sitting upright in a chair or lying on the floor. First, tense the muscles in the feet. Hold for a few seconds and then relax. Exhale as you relax. Repeat this same process with the ankles, calves, thighs, buttocks, abdomen, chest, arms and hands, back, shoulders, neck and facial muscles. After doing each part, then tense, hold and relax the muscles in the entire body. Do this a couple of times.

In her book Deborah Rozman (1976) describes different meditations that can be done with children. Below is one example:

> Another concentration exercise consists of concentrating on the second hand of a watch or clock as it circles around. Every time a thought enters, let it flow by, don't let it carry you away from your point of concentration. Each thought is like a fishhook trying to catch you, the fish. See how long you can concentrate without getting hooked into thinking about something else. (p. 102)

Rozman's suggestions are for elementary school children. If one is going to teach meditation to students at any level, of course it is important that the teacher be meditating.

In preparing to do any visualization, it is helpful to begin with a relaxation exercise. The student does the muscle relaxation exercise or some deep breathing. The teacher should also make it clear to students that there is not a right set of images but whatever comes into mind is appropriate and these images will vary with each student. Students should be encouraged to close their eyes during the experience since it is much more difficult to visualize with the eyes open. A few students may not be comfortable closing their eyes, however, and they should be allowed to keep their eyes open. Students should also be told that they are in charge of their own experience. If they feel uncomfortable at anytime they can open their eyes and stop the exercise for themselves.

In reading guided imagery exercises there are often pause signs (. . .) where you should allow approximately 5 to 10 seconds of silence. The whole idea is not to rush the experience. Depending on the exercise it can sometimes help the process by playing soft music in the background.

After the exercise there should always be some debriefing or follow-up activity. For example, students can write about their experiences in a journal or discuss their experiences with other students in small groups of three or four students. Guided imagery is most productive when it becomes part of the life of the classroom and is

[handwritten marginal notes: "journal", "Good creative writing activity"]

connected to ongoing curriculum. It is least helpful when it is used as a fill-in activity.

Finally below is an example from a secondary high school math teacher. It shows how the simplest form of meditation can be integrated into a classroom situation.

Idea for Alg A/ classes.

JUST ONE MINUTE

In a big inner-city public high school, in a Midwestern city, in my classroom, I start every class period with one minute of stillness. I am a mathematics teacher.

This began in the fall of 1997 with one particularly disruptive class. Out of not knowing how else to quiet things down, I started class one day talking about how we react to what goes on around us. We react to our friends, to the teachers, to each other. We react to the loud speakers, the classes next door, the commotion in the halls. We are bombarded by outside events. So I invited them to breathe in, straighten up the spine with feet flat on the floor, and be still for 60 seconds. Not to react to anything. I rang a bell, closed my eyes, and breathed. When one minute passed I rang the bell again, breathed slowly, thanked them for the minute in which they gave their best, and invited them to thank those nearby. From this spontaneous response to one difficult class, I have continued to start all my classes in the same way. This is the fifth year.

In the beginning, it was questionable as to whether the practice made much of an impact on that disruptive class. Some students humored me and others ignored me, but for that one minute the noise level reduced at least a notch, so I continued. Over time, more students started thanking each other. First in jest, they playfully said to each other they would try better next time, and so it went.

I maintained the process, yet I never once made reference to meditation. I could do with my own minute what I chose without imposing anything on the students, and many days I practiced metta. About a month into the practice, in the middle of a lesson, there was a particular outburst from a student whom I had to escort out of the classroom. When we returned to the lesson, another loud student commanded, "Ms. Baer, I think we need to do that minute thing again!" Vulnerable as I was, I closed my eyes in that class.

One day when I was delayed, a student spoke out, "Let's marinate," and rang the bells. Everyone did the one minute with him! From them on others wanted their turn to ring the bells. The noise and disturbances were reducing for the minute. The practice, however imperfect, gave even the most boisterous students a tool to use to settle the mind and body. I was convinced that it served not only me but the students as well.

In some of my advanced math classes, where discipline was not such an issue, there were mixed reactions. Most participated willingly in the minute of stillness, but a few were visibly uncomfortable and overtly resistant. I always thanked especially them for their minute of cooperation. Over time even these resistant ones became relaxed without having to work so hard at their resistance. It just was. A minute to do nothing.

This year one of my classes, mostly tenth graders, repeatedly requested to extend the minute of stillness even longer. So one day, with consent from everyone in the class, we did five minutes. When I rang the bell at the end, the stillness continued to linger. Wow! It was "awesome." They said they liked it when it was so quiet. They have continued to ask for more time, so we agreed to extend the minute on Fridays.

Our one minute has produced all sorts of responses. Once, a parent complained to the principal, who assured the parent it was appropriately secular if it came from me. Last spring as a student handed in his final exam before leaving for the summer, with tears of appreciation in his eyes, he thanked me for the daily minute. He said it meant a lot to him. This year three students from a class next door come daily to join my class for the minute, afterward thanking their buddies before returning to their own classroom. Parents of former students have come up to me in the grocery store to tell me how much their son or daughter appreciated that minute. They thanked me.

If nothing else, our 60 seconds has given me a degree more equanimity to start each class. That has been reason enough to continue. It was a huge challenge to accept the chaos in that first loud and disruptive class. But for just that one minute I told myself to let go of all my judgment—I am the responsible teacher, I have to keep order, it is my right and duty to judge and correct. I learned to accept just what is.

Over time the minute has softened me to my students. I have feelings of compassion for their being exactly where they are. Its authenticity comes across when I see little respectful responses, some thoughtfulness or a smile I would not have expected from them or from me. I continue to gain from our minute: to close my eyes and open my heart, to see the kindness that seeks an invitation to express itself from under the harsh exterior that circumstances have somehow created in my students. They show me myself. (Baer, 2003, p. 21)

Naomi refers to *metta,* which is a loving-kindness meditation. This meditation is described more fully in the next chapter.

REFERENCES

Baer, N. (2003). Just one minute. *Inquiring Mind: The Semiannual Journal of the Vipassana Community, 20*(1), 21.
Benson. H. (1976). *The relaxation response.* New York: Avon.
Carrington, P. (1977). *Freedom in meditation.* New York: Doubleday.
Easwaran, E. (1977). *The mantram handbook: Formulas for transformation.* Berkeley, CA: Nilgri Press.
Erriker, C., & Erriker, J. (Eds.). (2001). *Meditation in schools: Calmer classrooms.* New York: Continuum.
Frankl, V. (1992). *Man's search for meaning.* Boston: Beacon.
Goldstein, J. (1976). *The experience of insight: A natural unfolding.* Santa Cruz, CA: Unity Press.
Hart, W. (1987). *Vipassana meditation as taught by S. N. Goenka.* San Francisco: Harper.
Kabat-Zinn, J. (1990). *Full catastrophe living: Using the wisdom of your body and mind to face stress, pain and illness.* New York: Delacorte Press.
Krishnamurti, J. (1963). *Life ahead.* Wheaton, IL: Theosophical.
Leshan, L. (1974). *How to meditate.* Boston: Little, Brown.

Levete, G. (1995). *Presenting the case for meditation in primary and secondary schools.* Unpublished manuscript.

McLeod, K. (2001). *Wake up to your life: Discovering the Buddhist path of attention.* San Francisco: Harper.

Miller, J. (1993). *The holistic teacher.* Toronto: OISE Press.

Miller, J. (2000). *Education and the soul: Toward a spiritual curriculum.* Albany, NY: SUNY Press.

Miller, J., & Nozawa, A. (2002). Meditating teachers: A qualitative study. *Journal of Inservice Education, 28*(1),179–192.

Moyers, B. (1993). *Healing and the mind.* [Television series]. New York & Washington, DC: Public Broadcasting Service.

Murdoch, I. (1992). *Metaphysics as a guide to morals.* London: Chatto & Windus.

Murphy, M. (1992). *The future of the body: Explorations into the further evolution of human nature.* New York: Jeremy P. Tarcher.

Ram Dass. (1978). *Journey of awakening: A meditator's guidebook.* New York: Bantam.

Rozman, D. (1976). *Meditation for children.* Millbrae, CA: Celestial Arts.

Samuels, M., & Samuels, N. (1975). *Seeing with the mind's eye.* New York: Random House.

Savary, L. M., & Berne, P. H. (1988). *Kything: The art of spiritual presence.* Mahwah, NJ: Paulist Press.

Smith, H. (1986). *The religions of man.* New York: Harper Perennial.

Walsh, R. (1999). *Essential spirituality.* New York: John Wiley.

Williams, R. (1989). *The trusting heart: Great news about type A behavior.* New York: Time Books.

CHAPTER FIVE

Compassion, Caring, and Loving-Kindness

Love and compassion are necessities, not luxuries. Without them humanity cannot survive.

—Dalai Lama

Compassion and love are central to almost all religious and spiritual traditions. Christ said, "Do unto others as you would have them do unto you" (Luke 6:31, New Revised Standard Version), while the Buddha said that you should "consider others as yourself" (Dhammapada I0.1). However despite these universal teachings, compassion and love have made little headway into our schools. Nel Noddings (1992), who has written extensively on caring, has cited research that indicates that caring is not a priority in our schools. One study found that only "one third of the students in the Girl Scout survey said that their teachers care for them and that the proportion decreases as students get older" (p. 1). James Comer (1988) found that the single greatest complaint of students in large secondary schools is that the teachers don't care. The current emphasis on testing and individual competition leaves even less room for the compassion than when the studies cited above were done. The problem is not limited to education, as it tends to pervade Western society. Jeffrey Hopkins (2001) writes:

Based on my own experience, I have learned that from the infection of an attitude of "me against the world"—when the bottom line is SELF, SELF, SELF—either despair or merciless competitiveness erupts, undermining one's own happiness as well as that of everyone around us, rending asunder the fabric of society, the very basis of a happy life. . . . A compassionless perspective leads to the mania of thinking that mere economic success, while admittedly important, is the be-all and end-all of human existence; it gives rise to amoral and even immoral pursuit of money, in which one does not recognize the difference between adequate external facilities and true internal satisfaction. (p. 10)

KINDNESS, EMPATHY, COMPASSION, AND LOVE

Aldous Huxley, the novelist and philosopher, said at the end of his life, "It is a little embarrassing that, after forty-five years of research and study, the best advice I can give to people is to be a little kinder to each other" (cited in Sawyer, 2002, p. 190).

Kindness starts with the ability to see the needs and interests of others. This ability has been called empathy. Carl Rogers (1969) believed that empathy was one of the key elements in any helping relationship including teaching. He argued that, along with the ability to be genuine and convey respect, empathy was essential to effective teaching. Several studies cited by Rogers support this conclusion.

Empathy is intimately connected with compassion. In compassion we need to be able to see the others' points of view. However, compassion involves a stronger sense of identification with others. Compassion is rooted in seeing that we are all deeply interconnected. It is this sense of interconnection that is so fundamental to compassion. Through this sense of interconnection we realize that other beings like ourselves want relief from suffering and genuine happiness. We see this most directly with our family and friends but we can also realize that those that are far away from us geographically or emotionally also desire happiness and freedom from suffering. The Dalai Lama often begins his talks with the statement he feels he knows everyone in the audience like a brother or sister because he knows that they want happiness like himself. He feels that this more universal compassion is "unconditional, undifferentiated, and universal in scope" (1999, p. 123).

Thich Nhat Hanh makes the case that compassion is actually a verb, a movement of the heart (Salzberg, 1997, p. 130). Salzberg notes that the classic definition of compassion in Pali, the language of the Buddha, is that it is "the trembling or quivering of the heart" (p. 130). Implicit in this concept of compassion is not just a feeling or awareness but movement and action.

Love also involves this movement. The Buddha said "Just as a mother would protect her only child at the risk of her own life, even so cultivate a boundless heart toward all beings. Let your thoughts of boundless love pervade the whole world" (Sutta-Nipata I49–I50). Christ also spoke of universal love that can mean laying down one's life for one's friends (John 15:12–13).

Compassion and love are essential to timeless learning. Forgotten in the landscape of accountability and standardized tests, the compassionate or caring teachers are usually the teachers that we remember. The Dalai Lama (1995) notes:

> Of course, in the field of education, there is no doubt that compassionate motivation is important and relevant. Irrespective of whether you are a believer or non-believer, compassion for the students' lives futures, not only for their examinations, makes your work as a teacher much more effective. With that motivation, I think your students will remember you for the whole of their lives. (p. 72)

The rest of this chapter will explore various ways that we can nurture love and compassion in ourselves as teachers and in our students.

LOVING-KINDNESS PRACTICE

It is possible to make the development of compassion a living practice for both teachers and students. For example, there is a meditation that can cultivate this sense of compassion and it is called *loving-kindness* practice.

The essence of this meditation which is called *metta* in Pali is to center ourselves first in the heart area and to contact a basic warmth there. After connecting with the heart, we then attempt to share this warmth and energy with others. For example, one could use the following approach:

May I be well, happy, and peaceful.

May my family be well, happy, and peaceful.

May my friends be well, happy, and peaceful.

May my neighbors be well, happy, and peaceful.

May my colleagues be well, happy, and peaceful.

May all people whom I meet be well, happy, and peaceful.

May all people who may have injured me by deed, speech, or thought be well, happy, and peaceful.

May all beings on this planet be well, happy, and peaceful.

May all beings in this universe be well, happy, and peaceful.

This approach starts with those who are emotionally closest to us and then moves out from there. Another approach is to move out geographically:

May I be well, happy, and peaceful.

May all beings in this room be well, happy, and peaceful.

May all beings in this building be well, happy, and peaceful.

May all beings in this neighborhood be well, happy, and peaceful.

May all beings in this town or city be well, happy, and peaceful.

May all beings in this region be well, happy, and peaceful.

May all beings on this continent be well, happy, and peaceful.

May all beings in this hemisphere be well, happy, and peaceful.

May all beings in this planet be well, happy, and peaceful.

May all beings everywhere be well, happy, and peaceful.

The words can vary as you can wish—for the liberation of others or that they can gain more wisdom that frees them from suffering.

When you are doing lovingkindness, it is also possible to visualize the people whom you are sending these thoughts to. I start my classes with this exercise and I find that it has added immeasurably to the tone and feel of the class.

Several of my students have used it in their own lives. One student from Ghana likes to practice this when he sees people on the subway or bus:

> When I see people around, or when I move in the traffic it gives me the joy to meditate and [be] with those people . . . at times, you see some sad faces when you immediately enter public transit, and you have to meditate and wish them all well.

Another student from Panama also used it in a similar manner. "When I see each person in the subway, I look at them and pray for them. And I see a brother and a sister, and a family everywhere."

Metta comes from the Buddhist tradition but can be found in most religious and spiritual traditions. The Christian Monks of New Skete (1999) write about "benevolence—from the Latin *benevolentia,* meaning good will—means a universal disposition of good will towards others" (p. 242). The monks state that this is a spiritual practice which "takes the repeated, conscious decision or act of will to make this virtue a part of our life. It is very hard work" (p. 242). Yet to will the highest good for each person we meet, without exception "is the central struggle of an integrated spiritual practice" (p. 246).

As teachers we can visualize our students and send them thoughts of well-being. We can try to gain a sense of what they need at this point in their development and wish that for them.

CARING IN SCHOOLS

Nel Noddings (1984, 1992) is one of the leading authorities on encouraging educators to pursue caring as one of the main goals of education and schooling. She suggests that students can learn to care for themselves, others (both those close to them and people they do not know), plants and animals, and ideas. She offers a comprehensive approach which she summarizes in the following way:

1. Be clear and unapologetic about our goal. The main aim of education should be to produce competent, caring, loving, and lovable people.

2. Take care of the need for affiliation.
   - Keep students and teachers together (by mutual consent) for several years.
   - Keep students together where possible.
   - Keep them in the same building for considerable periods of time.
   - Help students to think of the school as *theirs.*
   - Legitimize time spent in building relations of care and trust.

3. Relax the impulse to control.
   - Give teachers and students more responsibility to exercise judgment.
   - Get rid of competitive grading.
   - Reduce testing and use a few well-designed tests to assess whether people can handle the tasks they want to undertake competently.
   - Encourage teachers to explore with students. We don't have to know everything to teach well.
   - Define expertise more broadly and instrumentally. For example, a biology teacher should be able to teach whatever mathematics is involved in biology.
   - Encourage self-evaluation.
   - Involve students in governing their own classrooms and schools.
   - Accept the challenge to care by teaching well the things students want to learn.

4. Get rid of program hierarchies. This will take time, but we must begin now to provide an excellent program for *all* our children. Programs for the non-college-bound should be just as rich, desirable, and rigorous as those for the college-bound.
   - Abandon uniform requirements for college entrance. What a student wants to do or to study should guide what is required by way of preparation.
   - Give all students what all students need: genuine opportunities to explore the questions central to human life.

5. Give at least part of every day to themes of care.

   – Discuss existential questions freely, including spiritual matters.

   – Help students to treat each other ethically. Give them practice in caring.

   – Help students to understand how groups and individuals create rivals and enemies. Help them to learn how to "be on both sides."

   – Encourage a way of caring for animals, plants, and the environment that is consistent with caring for humans.

   – Encourage caring for the human-made world. Help students to be at home in technical, natural, and cultural worlds. Cultivate wonder and appreciation for the human-made world.

6. Teach them that caring in every domain implies competence. When we care, we accept the responsibility to work continuously on our own competence so that the recipient of our care—person, animal, object, or idea—is enhanced. There is nothing mushy about caring. It is the strong, resilient backbone of human life. (pp. 174–175)

This is a very comprehensive approach to caring in schools and deserves careful consideration by administrators and teachers. I have written in other contexts (Miller, 2000) how taking care of plants, animals, and the earth can be very important to nurturing the souls of students. One of the most interesting examples comes from the work of my colleagues in Japan.

School With Forest and Meadow (Ojiya School)

When I was in Japan in 1994 I had the opportunity to visit a school that demonstrated this sense of caring and reverence. This school called Ojiya School is described in detail by Ikue Tezuka (1995) in a book entitled *School With Forest and Meadow*.

This school is fortunate to be situated on large grounds. The school itself is rectangular and encircles an open area that is called the "Friendship Pasture." Living in this pasture are a variety of animals including goats, chickens, rabbits, and turtles. The pasture is a 440-square-meter pen surrounded by a net which was made with the help of parents and teachers. When the weather is good, the animals are let out to feed on the grounds. The children love to go into the pasture to "touch, hold, speak to, and take care of the animals" (p. 3). Tezuka, who visited the school on several occasions, writes, "One can observe the children growing in love and gentleness through taking care of their animal friends" (p. 4). When I walked into the pasture during my visit, my first impression was of three boys on a bench each holding and petting a rabbit, confirming Tezuka's remarks.

Tezuka (1995) reports that, at first, many children were afraid of the animals. Many students did not like the chickens which they felt were dirty and smelled bad. But gradually they began to change their attitude on closer acquaintance. "Now the children run to the pens and buildings at cleaning time in the morning. They look forward to taking care of the rabbits. They even like to clean the hen house" (p. 5). The students have come "to sympathize with these creatures and sense their own kinship with them" (p. 6).

The school also has a small forest called "Yasho Homeland Forest" with about 300 trees. Before the students and teachers planted the trees, they surveyed the surrounding area and identified all the different kinds of native trees. They found 96 different kinds of trees and shrubs within 10 kilometers of the school. In planting the trees, attention was given to the size and colors of the flowers and buds, incorporating consideration of aesthetic principles into the learning of natural science. Tezuka describes how the forest changes colors through the seasons. In spring there are red blossoms which grow against the green background. In summer the variety of colors increases with whites, more reds, and purples appearing. In fall, of course, the leaves on the trees turn orange and yellow.

The students are very concerned about the trees. If there is a typhoon, the first thing they do is look at the trees to see if they are alright when they come the next day. The students write about their feelings for the trees in poems (Tezuka, 1995, pp. 10–11):

Trees in the Home Forest

I saw trees in the ground.
They are moving as if they were dancing with snow.

Don't they feel heavy
When they have snow on their branches!

—Yukari Kazama

Trees

I saw trees.
They look as if they were weeping in the snow.
Don't they feel pain when they are bound with ropes?
I'd like to remove the ropes to make them feel better.

—Takumi Yokota

Home Forest

Trees in Home Forest.
Dead Trees.
They are covered with snow.
They look as if they were saying, "It's cold."
They seem to be saying to the neighboring trees:
"It's cold" "I hope spring comes soon."
The trees are good friends.

—Rie Sato

The poems are evidence that children at Ojiya School are learning a deep reverence for the natural world. They are also gaining in their knowledge of the principles of conservation as they progress with their care of the trees. For example, when fall came, they used to put the fallen leaves in a bag for disposal, and now they put the leaves under the trees to help enrich the soil there.

The person responsible for the approach at Ojiya School is Giichiro Yamanouchi, a former principal. He felt that a forest could provide many learning opportunities for children and also foster their ability to take care of the natural environment around them. He believed that it would be useful for learning science and writing compositions as well as other learning activities. He thinks that the forest is also good for the children's souls. He found that the children liked to go to the forest to be alone, sit quietly, and listen to the forest. He calls these forests "natural meditation rooms" where the child's soul can be nourished.

The forest also stimulates self-directed learning activity. One child who had never made any initiative on his own became more alert and wrote a five-page composition about the forest. Another child became more observant of birds in the area as a result of the forest:

Birds and the Protection of Nature

Isn't nature the most important thing for us? But if it is being lost, how can we learn about it? From newspapers? On TV? These tell us about the destruction of nature as news, after it happens. Then it is almost too late to do anything. Isn't there some way in which we can learn about these things sooner, before nature is destroyed? One way that I thought of was to observe living creatures because they are nature itself. So I began to observe birds as a kind of "barometer." I compared the numbers and kinds of birds I observed in three areas in Nagaoka city: in front of the station, around this school and on the Shinano river.

There were only 5 species in front of the station; dove, starling, swallow, sparrow, and crow. Around the school, I observed 23 species and on the Shinano River there were 33 different kinds of birds: 6 species of heron, 13 of duck and goose, 7 of eagle and hawk, and 7 of snipe. There is a big difference in the number of species in the 3 places.

I compared not only the number but the nature of the birds. In front of the station, there were only birds which can live in crowded, noisy places. Around the school, there were birds which do not like noisy places and can live only in residential areas. If the whole of Nagaoka city becomes like the area around the station, what will happen to the birds?

Then, how about planting more trees like Kawasaki Forest? Birds will surely be attracted to them. Planting trees helps to protect nature. The protection of nature is not only monitoring national parks but also doing more common things such as making a wooden path in Kawasaki Forest, studying about trees in it, taking care of them, and not filling the Suyoshi River with

dirty water. We should develop this kind of attitude if we want
to protect nature.

—Takeshi Morohashi
(cited inTezuka, 1995, pp. 60–61)

Clearly this student is learning reverence for the natural world
and is taking some form of action to preserve it.

Parents also became convinced of the value of the forest project.
Their enthusiasm prompted them to help raise money for the forest.
In all the schools where he has served as principal, Yamanouchi
worked with parents and community members to help the school.
One of his schools was located in a community where raising carp
was a local industry. He was able to persuade a person who raised
the expensive fish to donate some to the school. The children again
learned how to take care of these fish and the donation of the fish
created a lot of community interest in the school.

I have met and worked with Yamanouchi and he is one of the
most interesting and passionate educators I have ever met. Although
he is retired now, he is still very active and extremely energetic.
Recently he won an award for his work, and a day of celebration was
held in his honor in June 2004. My wife and I attended this day
where former students and parents commented on the impact of having a small forest on the school grounds. One parent got up and
talked about how an experience with his daughter at the school had
a profound impact on him. One day he went with her to school to
look at the tree she was taking care of. There was a small vine growing around the bottom of the tree and the father started to remove it.
His daughter got upset and said: "Don't do that! The vine and the
tree are friends." The father said that his daughter's words hit him
like a hammer and since that moment he has looked on the natural
world in a different way. He said he is much more sensitive to the
environment in his work in construction.

Tezuka (1995), in concluding her book, comments on
Yamanouchi's work: "Through the work of such dedicated people as
Giichiro Yamanouchi, amazing things are beginning to happen. . . .
There is developing a ground swell movement toward holistic student-
centered education in our country" (p. 88).

In North America there is a movement to have a garden in every
school. In the book *Digging Deeper* Joseph Kiefer and Martin Kemple

(1998) provide examples of many different types of gardens that students can grow. Students can also learn how to grow food as well as take care of plants. Like the example from Japan, this approach fosters the connection between children and other living creatures.

SERVICE LEARNING

Service learning involves students in a community activity that is also linked to academic work in the school. I would like to cite a couple of examples of service learning from two of my friends and colleagues, John Donnelly and Lourdes Arguelles.

Engaged Service

Engaged service is the term that John Donnelly uses to describe the work he does with at-risk adolescents. The goal of this work is development of compassion in students or the ability to see that another person's suffering is not separate from ourselves. The teachings of Ram Dass have had a strong impact on John and he quotes Ram Dass's (Ran Dass & Bush, 1992) definition of compassion:

> Compassion in action is paradoxical and mysterious. It is absolute, yet continually changing. It accepts that everything is happening exactly as it should, and it works with a full-hearted commitment to change. It sets goals but knows that the process is all there is. It is joyful in the midst of suffering and hopeful in the face of overwhelming odds. It is simple in a world of complexity and confusion. It is done for others but nurtures the self. (pp. 3–5)

Engaged service, then, is a process of attempting to heal this suffering in others and ourselves. John Donnelly likes to use nature and field trips to the outdoors to engage his students. Yet these are not just trips to see and observe nature; they also involve students helping one another. Donnelly (2002) described one of activities that his students engaged in:

> On one occasion during field trip, ten of my students helped one student who was confined to a wheelchair gain mobility around a mountain camp that had not been adapted for children with specific physical needs. They assisted him off the bus, folded his

wheelchair, set out his silverware at the table, and by splitting into three different teams, helped him hike on trails that were inaccessible to children with special needs. They finished a full day of these activities by helping him get ready and go to bed. . . . I doubt if any more love or concern could be shown by a group of students. (p. 310)

Many of the students in this program come from extremely challenging backgrounds. One of his students was shot on the streets of Los Angeles. Yet John with this love and commitment has been able to bring hope to many of his students. He remains hopeful that we can offer an education that is truly life affirming. He writes: "Look to the children and they will show us the way. Ask them what they need, do not explain to them what they want. Ask them how they can help, do not tell them what is required. Make the subject of the day a life that can be enhanced" (Donnelly, 2002, p. 314).

Community-Based Work

Lourdes Arguelles teaches at Claremont Graduate School in California. Her students range in age from their mid-20s to mid-50s. As part of the curriculum she has them go into grassroots communities which are often marginalized, either economically or socially. First, she has her students just be with people in these communities in informal situations such as "sharing meals and casual conversation, and doing manual labor" (Arguelles, 2002, p. 294). Second, she encourages "slow, non-deliberate, non-formal and sporadic ways of knowing" which she calls "slow mind" (p. 296). For some students the shift to slow mind was a challenge as one student said: "When I first met my teacher I was not as ready for sustained and formal interaction with her as I am now. My mind was too accelerated. The time I have taken just talking and being with people at a low-income housing project sort of settled me in, and I formed a bond with the other students and with the teacher in addition to the bonds with the people in the community. I also began to realize how some of the things that I do in my classroom and in my life can impact negatively on the lives of these people. That has made a real difference in my life and in my teaching" (p. 295).

Lourdes offers a course that challenges her students in many different ways. Through these challenges they find ways to connect more deeply with themselves and others.

TO BE AND TO HAVE

At the heart of any program is the way that the teachers treat each other and the students. One of the best examples of caring for students can be seen in the recent movie *Etre et Avoir* (*To Be and to Have*). This movie shows a teacher in rural France, Georges Lopez, in a small school in his last year of teaching. At first one is struck by the traditional form of teaching he employs; for example, he dictates readings to the students. However, he deals with every situation and student with total attention and care. One student, a girl in Grade 6, Nathalie, is so shy she is almost mute. At the end of the film she is sitting with the teacher on the doorsteps of the school and they are talking about how she will do in the new school next year. He explores her communication difficulties in the most gentle manner and suggests to her that if she wants she can visit him on Saturdays. The girl is trying to hold back her tears. This is one of the most moving scenes I have seen in any movie, much less a movie about education. Yet it comes from the depth of the teacher's caring about this student. One film reviewer, Rob Thomas (2004), summarizes my own feelings:

> With his university goatee and stern gaze, Lopez at first seems like a strict taskmaster. . . . But we quickly understand that Lopez is a great teacher in every sense of the word, drawing from infinite reserves of patience and respect as he instructs his pupils, never raising his voice, never talking down to even the youngest student. . . . His teaching is simply one of the purest expressions of love I've ever seen on film.

Lopez provides an example that many of us can follow. His strong loving presence conveys what is really important in teaching. I will have more to say about presence in the next chapter.

REFERENCES

Arguelles, L. (2002). How do we live, learn and die: How a teacher and some of her students meditated and walk on an engaged Buddhist path. In J. P. Miller and Y. Nakagawa (Eds.), *Nurturing our wholeness: Perspectives on spirituality in education* (pp. 285–303). Brandon, VT: Foundation for Educational Renewal.

Comer, J. (1988). Is "parenting" essential to good teaching? *NEA Today, 6,* 34–40.

Dalai Lama. (1995). *The power of compassion.* San Francisco: Thorsons.

Dalai Lama. (1999). *Ethics for the new millennium.* New York: Penguin.

The Dhammapada: With introductory essays, Pali text, English translation and notes (S. Radakrishnan, Trans.). (1996). London: Oxford University Press.

Donnelly, J. (2002). Educating for a deeper sense of self: Understanding compassion and engaged service. In J. P. Miller and Y. Nakagawa (Eds.), *Nurturing our wholeness: Perspectives on spirituality in education* (pp. 304–317). Brandon, VT: Foundation for Educational Renewal.

Hopkins, J. (2001). *Cultivating compassion: A Buddhist perspective.* New York: Broadway Books.

Kiefer, J., & Kemple, M. (1998). *Digging deeper: Integrating youth gardens into schools & communities.* Philadelphia, PA: American Community Gardening Association.

Miller, J. (2000). *Education and the soul: Toward a spiritual curriculum.* Albany, NY: SUNY Press.

Monks of New Skete. (1999). *In the spirit of happiness.* Boston: Little, Brown.

Noddings, N. (1984) *Caring: A feminine approach to ethics and moral education.* Berkeley, CA: University of California Press.

Noddings, N. (1992) *The challenge to care in schools: An alternative approach to education.* New York: Teachers College Press.

Ram Dass, & Bush, M. (1992). *Compassion in action: Setting out on the path of service.* New York: Bell Tower.

Rogers, C. (1969). *Freedom to learn.* Columbus, OH: Charles Merrill.

Salzberg, S. (1997). *A heart as wide as the world: Living with mindfulness, wisdom, and compassion.* Boston: Shambhala.

Sawyer, D. (2002). *Aldous Huxley: A biography.* New York: Crossroad.

The Sutta-Nipata (H. Saddhatissa, Trans.). (1985). London: Curzon Press.

Tezuka, I. (1995). *School with forest and meadow.* San Francisco: Caddo Gap Press.

Thomas, R. (2004). [Review of the motion picture *To Be and to Have*]. Retrieved March 17, 2005, from www.rottentomatoes.com

CHAPTER SIX

Contemplation, Mindfulness, and Presence

Contemplation is the highest expression of man's intellectual and spiritual life. It is that life itself, fully active, fully aware that it is alive. It is spiritual wonder. It is spontaneous awe at the sacredness of life, of being. It is gratitude for life, for awareness and for being.

—Thomas Merton, 1972, p. 1

Dante also recognized the importance of contemplation. At the end of his long journey in *The Divine Comedy* he reaches Saturn, the last and highest of the planets. It is here where the souls of the contemplatives reside. Helen Luke in her wonderful book on *The Divine Comedy* (1989) writes: "Dante is the poet of contemplation, not as opposed to action, the value of which he constantly asserts, but in the sense of seeing, understanding, contemplating with insight, that which is behind all action and gives it its only meaning" (p. 167).

Most spiritual and religious traditions have spoken of this different way of knowing: contemplation. As stated in the beginning of this book the traditional way of learning in schools has been to acquire factual knowledge and a few skills (transmission). In some cases learning has moved beyond this to include analysis and problem solving (transaction). However, in both these cases the subject (the learner) remains separate from the material to be learned or analyzed;

in short the learning is dualistic. Dualistic learning has an important place in schools; however, education has ignored nondualistic forms of learning which are often found in various spiritual and religious traditions.

When we contemplate something, the boundary between ourselves and whatever we are contemplating disappears. Luke (1989) cites Krishnamurti in defining contemplation: "When you look totally you will give your whole attention, your whole being, everything of yourself, your eyes, your ears, your nerves. You will attend with complete self abandonment" (p. 167). John Welwood (2000) refers to contemplation as "unconditional presence." He writes: "Unconditional presence is the most powerful transmuting force there is—precisely because it is willingness to be there with our experience, without dividing ourselves in two by trying to 'manage' what we are feeling" (p. 101). Welwood cites Tarthang Tulku (1974) to give an example of presence and the contemplative state:

> Just be there. . . .You become the center of thought. But there is not really any center—the center becomes balance. There's no 'being,' no 'subject-object relationship': none of these categories exist. Yet at the same time there is . . . complete openness. (pp. 9–10)

Welwood and Tulku are writing from a Buddhist perspective but consider also the words of the Monks of New Skete (1999) who are Christian: "The true contemplative is the one who lives in balance. . . ." "Being happy means entering wholeheartedly into everything—no matter what the possible difficulties. We have to enter into it in such a way that we're no longer separated from what we're doing. We *forget* ourselves at the same time that we give ourselves completely" (pp. 270, 311).

MINDFULNESS

Welwood suggests that mindfulness is close to unconditional presence. Mindfulness is a form of meditation practice applied to everyday life and involves bringing awareness to acts that we do each moment. The rush and noise of our world makes it difficult to be fully present. For example, we may try to relax by going for a walk, but we often take our problems with us on the walk. We can take with us a problem at work or our concern over how to pay our bills, and we find at the end of our walk we were so preoccupied that we were not present to nature or ourselves. We haven't really felt the air on our face, or looked at the trees, or felt the warmth of the sun. Nature can be very healing as we experience it directly, but our thoughts get in the way. At times our preoccupations and thoughts can be a barrier to the world.

Another example of how it is difficult to be mindful is trying to do several things at once. At home I can be watching television, reading the paper, and trying to carry on a conversation with my wife. In our attempts to fit everything in, our consciousness becomes fragmented; our presence is diminished.

Another word for mindfulness is wholeheartedness. When we do something we enter into it completely. Because mindfulness is so important to reconnecting ourselves with the world around us, I encourage my students to work on being mindful. There are many simple exercises that we can do to be more present.

We can start our practice by focusing on doing one thing at a time. The whole experience of preparing a meal, eating, and doing the dishes can be done mindfully. For example, as you cut the celery for the salad, just cut the celery. Sometimes we can be so preoccupied that we can cut ourselves, rather than the celery. Gradually we find that by just cutting the celery we can do more to heal ourselves and the world. Being fully present is a profoundly healing act. As we eat the meal, we can also focus our attention on the eating, chewing, and swallowing. Often we read the paper or watch TV while we eat our meals and as a result we taste very little. Finally, when doing the dishes focus on the task. Feel the water as it cascades over your hands and the dishes. Often we can hardly wait to finish one task so that we can do something else. For example, as I do the dishes my mind will be on the hockey game which is about to start on TV. As I watch the hockey game, my mind begins to drift to problems that I may face at work tomorrow. As we do one thing, our mind is on another; we seem to live in the future or the past.

One master of mindfulness is Thich Nhat Hanh, the Vietnamese Buddhist monk, who has written several books on mindfulness. He suggests a variety of exercises in mindfulness and below is one example:

A Slow Motion Bath

Allow yourself 30 to 45 minutes to take a bath. Don't hurry for even one second. From the moment you prepare the bath water to the moment you put on clean clothes, let every motion be light and slow. Be attentive of every movement. Place your attention to every part of your body, without discrimination or fear. Be mindful of each stream of water on your body. By the time you've finished, your mind should feel as peaceful and light as your body. Follow your breath. Think of yourself as being in a clean and fragrant lotus pond in the summer. (Hanh, 1976, pp. 86–87)

I suggest that you start with very simple activities in developing mindfulness. Gradually you can then bring your attention to more complex situations. Mindfulness becomes a powerful way that we can carry our contemplative awareness into daily life. With mindfulness, meditation is not something that is fragmented or separated from the rest of life; instead, our day becomes a seamless whole of awareness. We find that we live in the most empowering place, the eternal now.

Several students in my class have found mindfulness a powerful practice. One student made it the main practice in her home life. She began the practice because her husband commented once that it must be painful to listen to him. She resolved to listen completely to her husband and children when they spoke to her. In referring to listening to her children, she wrote: "Each time that I stopped what I was doing to listen to them, they seemed surprised, and then delighted, that I had time for them." After a week or so she noticed that the "noise level in our house had diminished considerably. . . . I felt a calmness in our home that had not been there before." She also attempted to be nonjudgmental when people spoke to her. She quickly noticed that she often entered to conversations with expectations of what people were going to say. Letting go of these expectations and assumptions also had a very positive impact on her relationships with her husband and children.

Another student spoke about awe she felt when she contemplated on her children:

The impact on me is very powerful. I remember one day that I just watched my kids. I watched them sleeping, I observed them, for so long. I looked at their eyes, nose, hair . . . they look like angels. . . . Sometimes I just sit down outside and look at the skies. . . . I remember that everything is grace.

She describes that her change comes from inside and how mindfulness has affected her:

I hear sounds that I never heard. I hear the animals, I listen to everything that is there, that I never paid attention to before. I touch and feel . . . I know that I'm living and I don't have a word to express what this means to me really.

Mindfulness practice also affected how one of my students, Astrid De Cairos, approached her teaching day:

I began each day marveling at the miracle of life, of falling asleep and awakening to a wondrous world. With this thought, I began my morning rituals. Thinking of my daily routines as rituals actually helped me in attaining a more aware state as I washed my face, took my shower, ate my breakfast and walked (or drove) to work. Upon entering the school, I decided to go to my classroom first. I had previously been going into the office to sign in and say good morning, etc., but this took away from the oneness that I needed in my "mindfulness" training. I ritualized all my tasks—walking up the stairs, putting the key into the classroom door, hanging up my coat, etc. It was actually amazing how being mindful of these simple tasks allowed me to begin my day in a calm clear and less cluttered way. How many times had I come into this room, dumped my coat, hat and mitts on my chair, ran to the photocopy room and back, spent another half hour looking for the photocopying I had laid down somewhere, not to mention the frantic search for mitts when it was time go out on duty? Instead, I began to become aware of my mornings in the classroom and in turn they became calm and focused.

My most favorite part of this pre-school ritual is writing the schedule on the board. My team teacher had tried to talk me out of this last June (she writes the daily schedule for each day on the sheets of chart paper and laminates them). At the time, I explained to her that writing of the schedule on the board had many different purposes for me. The most important one was that it allowed me to center myself in the classroom. I look back now on how intuitive I had been and I am amazed. Being mindful of this particular ritual has made me fully aware of the "here" during the hectic day. I stand at the front of the room and feel the smooth texture of the chalk in my hands. I think about where I am and I observe my surroundings—the plants, the books, the desks, the children's slippers—I am, for the second time that day, amazed at the miracle of life.

The days begins, I stand outside the classroom fully aware of each individual as they enter the room. I interact with them, I say hello, it feels good. This is new, until now, I had never made it to the door when the children entered—I was always too busy! I try to maintain this sense of awareness—aware of my feelings (physical and emotional) and my reactions to the things that are happening 'now.' Of course, the craziness of the classroom day begins and it becomes more and more difficult to maintain this awareness as the day wears on. However, now instead of working through recess, I take the time to visit with colleagues in the staff room. When I can, I take a walk down to the beach at lunch and look out across the lake, mindful of the beauty of the world around me. When the day ends, I recapture this mindful state and fully participate in the end-of-day ritual with my students. After the children have left, I sweep the floor, being mindful of my movements and the sound of the broom. I often begin by thinking that I am sweeping the day's events away and that I am focusing on the 'now'—the actual act of sweeping. The pleasure of being here, and being able to fully participate reminds me again of the miracle of life.

One of the students who teaches music education at the university level taught mindfulness practice to his students. He believes that mindfulness practice can help his students approach mundane tasks in a way that makes them engage these activities more fully:

I'm encouraging my classes, pre-service teachers to take joy in the tasks that are not necessarily glamorous. You've got to count the number of reeds you have for your woodwind instruments. You've got to count the pages of music you count out to kids. This ultimately brings you happiness.

Mindfulness as taught by Thich Nhat Hanh and others comes from the Buddhist tradition, but consider again the teachings of the Monks of New Skete (1999):

> The way we work can change our state of mind. If we clean house conscientiously, even lovingly, our spiritual intentions become evident and are reinforced, and anxieties and petty concerns are put in perspective. . . . Don't fight the task; just carefully and calmly do good work, simply because the house needs to be clean. When your attention strays, focus again on the task at hand, for the quality of your work is also slipping. This exercise results in the satisfaction of having an orderly and clean house, and though you may be tired, you might even feel psychologically refreshed. In the very doing of this, you will experience how even this facet of life is worthy of respect. When you apply this to whatever your life asks of you, your attitude toward everything is transformed. (pp. 274–275)

Mindfulness and contemplation are different from *reflection*. They do not ask the teacher to reflect on something but simply be with the object. Teaching can move back and forth between mindfulness and reflection. Reflection allows us to step back to analyze what we have been doing; mindfulness and contemplation just let us be in the present moment. One way of looking at teaching is the movement back and forth between mindfulness and reflection. Both are essential to good teaching.

PRESENCE

The presence that the teacher displays is fundamental to teaching. In fact, if we recall the teachers who have had an impact on us, it is often not the material that they taught that we remember but that presence which somehow touched us deeply.

Shunryu Suzuki tells a wonderful story about the presence of a teacher. He was head of a temple in Japan and was looking for a kindergarten teacher for the temple school. He repeatedly tried to convince a woman to take the job but she refused. Finally he said to her, "You don't have to do anything, just stand there." When he said that, she accepted the position. He was convinced that her presence alone would make a difference in the lives of the children. Of course, teaching is not limited to presence; it also includes the skills and understandings that we bring to our work.

Emerson in talking to teachers emphasized the importance of presence in teaching:

> By your own act you teach the beholder how to do the practicable. According to the depth from which you draw your life, such is the depth not only of your strenuous effort, but of your manners and presence. The beautiful nature of the world has here blended your happiness with your power. . . . Consent yourself to be an organ of your highest thought, and lo! suddenly you put all men in your debt, and are the fountain of an energy that goes pulsing on with waves of benefit to the borders of society, to the circumference of things. (cited in Jones, 1966, p. 227)

CONTEMPLATION AND MINDFULNESS IN CLASSROOMS

I have already given some examples of bringing meditation into the classroom in Chapter 4 and I would like to discuss a few others here. First we can do some of the activities Thich Nhat Hanh suggested above.

Activities which can be done with students of almost all ages can focus on the senses. For example, take your students on a walk in nature and have them look, touch, and smell. I love the poem written by Walt Whitman entitled, "There Was a Child Went Forth":

> There was a child went forth each day,
>
> And the first object he look'd upon, that object he became,
>
> and that object became part of him for the day or a
>
> certain part of the day,
>
> Or for many years or stretching cycles of years.
>
> (1993, p. 57)

Whitman then goes on to describe all the plants (e.g., morning glories, clover, water-plants, field sprouts, apple trees), animals (fish, lambs, the phoebe-bird), aspects of nature (clouds, waves, the salt marsh), and people (teachers, other children, parents) that the child encounters during the day and how they become part of him or her. Whitman is describing how children learn through contemplation and mindfulness and captures the sense of wonder that the child carries in this process.

Whitman provides a powerful model for timeless learning that others have followed. Gloria Castillo (1974) in her book *Left-Handed Teaching* describes many activities that allow the child to become what he or she encounters. She suggests some rainy-day activities that include concentrating on the sound of rain, then drawing the rain, and dancing the rain. She suggests having the students watch raindrops sliding down the windowpanes and then having them imagine that they are raindrops. They then can write about their journey beginning with the phrase "I am a raindrop." Students can write words that describe the rain and how they feel about the rain. From these words they can write a poem or story about the rain.

Visualization, which was described in the chapter on attention, is also a method for allowing the student to contemplate. One of my favorite activities is "The Water Cycle" by Jack Sequist (cited in Miller, 2000, pp. 58–59). Here the student imagines water evaporating, becoming a cloud, and then coming down as snow and rain. This visualization encourages the student to have an inner experience that is often taught as something entirely external to the student.

Beverly-Collene Gaylean (1983) in her book *Mindsight* has developed a large number of imagery activities. She has created these activities for almost every subject area as well as in the more general area of personal development. Maureen Murdock (1982) has also written a book entitled *Spinning Inward* that is focused toward the elementary school student.

Another good book with many activities is *What We May Be* by Piero Ferrucci (1982). Below is a visualization more appropriate for older students:

The Sky

Imagine that it's a summer afternoon and you are lying on the grass. You feel the softness of the grass under you. Lying on your back, you look up at the sky: limpid, uncontaminated, deeply blue. Spend some time contemplating it.

You see a butterfly cross your field of vision. As it flies above you, you notice how light it seems and how delicately colored its wings are. Then you watch it disappear.

Now you see, silhouetted against the sky, an eagle high in flight. Following the eagle with your eyes, you penetrate the blue depths of the sky.

Still looking at the sky, you project your sight even higher. You can now see, very high and far way, a small white cloud pass. Watch it as it slowly dissolves.

Finally, there is only the boundless sky.

Become the sky—immaterial, immemorial, all inclusive. As the sky, realize that there are no limits. Realize that you are everywhere, reaching all, pervading everything. (p. 124)

CONTEMPLATION AND ACTION

As noted at the beginning of this chapter, contemplation and action are connected. Michael Dallaire, who has worked as an ecumenical chaplain in public housing projects and as a secondary school chaplain, develops the case for what he calls *contemplation-in-liberating praxis*. In Dallaire's view (2001) contemplation is linked with work for transformation and social justice. With regard to contemplation, he encourages solitude, meditation, awareness of emotions and the body, celebration, and play within community. Liberating praxis can be fostered through solidarity with others, dialogue, social action, and reflection on action. Dallaire sees the relationship between contemplation and liberating praxis as an interactive dialectic. He sees the teacher as a "radical, a transformative and public intellectual, and a prophet. They will teach for an alternative 'way of being in the world'" (p. 135). Teachers will view their relationship with students as "a partnership in pursuit of contemplation and reflective actions that liberate" (p. 136). The engaged service work of Arguelles and Donnelly described in the last chapter are good examples of contemplation-in-liberating praxis.

REFERENCES

Castillo, G. (1974). *Left-handed teaching.* New York: Praeger.

Dallaire, M. (2001). *Contemplation in liberation—A method of spiritual education in the schools.* Lewiston, NY: Edwin Mellen.

Ferucci, P. (1982). *What we may be: Techniques for psychological and spiritual growth.* Los Angeles: Jeremy P. Tarcher.

Gaylean, B. (1983). *Mindsight: Learning through imaging.* Healdsburg, CA: Center for Integrative Learning.

Hanh, T. N. (1976). *The miracle of mindfulness: A manual on meditation.* Boston: Beacon Press.

Hanh, T. N. (1991). *Peace is every step: The path of mindfulness in everyday life.* New York: Bantam.

Jones, H. M. (1966). *Emerson on education: Selections.* New York: Teachers College Press.

Luke, H. (1989). *Dark wood to white rose: Journey and transformation in Dante's Divine Comedy.* New York: Parabola.

Merton, T. (1972). *New seeds of contemplation.* New York: New Directions.

Miller, J. P. (2000). *Education and the soul: Toward a spiritual curriculum.* Albany, NY: SUNY Press.

Monks of New Skete. (1999). *In the spirit of happiness.* Boston: Little, Brown.

Murdock, M. (1982). *Spinning inward: Using guided imagery with children.* Culver City, CA: Peace Press.

Tulku, T. (1974). On thoughts. *Crystal Mirror, 3,* 7–20.

Welwood, J. (2000). Reflection and awakening: The dialectic of awakening. In T. Hart, P. L. Nelson, & K. Puhakka (Eds.), *Transpersonal knowing: Exploring the horizon of consciousness* (pp. 85–112). Albany, NY: SUNY Press.

Whitman, W. (1993). *From this soil: Selected poems by Walt Whitman* (C. Gudis, Ed.). New York: The Nature Company.

PART III

Timeless Learning: Perspectives, Examples, and Outcomes

CHAPTER SEVEN

Educational Perspectives on Timeless Learning

> *To Teach, with reference to Eternity.*
>
> —Bronson Alcott

This chapter examines three broad approaches to timeless learning, while the following chapter looks at examples of schools that have a timeless quality. Transcendental Education, Holistic Education, and Slow Education are the perspectives that are discussed here. Transcendental Education was articulated by the American transcendentalists of the 19th century: namely, Emerson, Thoreau, and Bronson Alcott. Emerson's writing has been called timeless (Cromphout, 2003) because he addressed "the timeless human search for self-definition" (p. 7). Holistic Education has roots that can be traced back to Greece and to indigenous peoples, and it also has a timeless quality. It recognizes that within a person there is an unconditioned, timeless element (i.e., the soul) that needs to be nourished and sustained if we truly want to educate the whole person. Slow Education, a more recent phenomenon, has arisen out of the slow food movement and encourages educators to engage in learning with greater depth.

TRANSCENDENTAL EDUCATION

> *A moment is a concentrated eternity.*
>
> —Emerson (1996, p. 116)

Keep the time—observe the hours of the universe—not of the cars. What are 3 score years & ten hurriedly & coarsely lived to moments of divine leisure, in which your life is coincident with the life of the Universe?

—Thoreau (cited in Bickman, 1999, p. 49)

Ralph Waldo Emerson, Henry David Thoreau, and Bronson Alcott were associated with the transcendentalist movement in 19th-century America. Transcendentalism was not really a movement in the true sense of the term. Perhaps the only idea that linked people to this term was the belief that our best moments come when we listen to our consciences, or the still small voice within, rather than following the expectations of society. Other individuals associated with transcendentalism include Margaret Fuller and Walt Whitman. Lawrence Buell (1973) characterizes transcendentalism in the following way: "Transcendentalism can almost be said to have begun as a discussion group. Much of its internal ferment and a good deal of its external impact can be attributed to talkers like Alcott and Fuller; even its writing is largely oral literature in the sense of having been composed originally for the pulpit or the lyceum" (p. 77). Bickman (2004) suggests that these conversations were *continuing* education in the best sense (p. 62).

Emerson and Henry Thoreau are among the most important writers in American letters. Bronson Alcott was a close friend to both of these men when they all lived in Concord, Massachusetts, and was the person most interested in education; however, both Thoreau and Emerson were teachers and wrote about education.

Emerson

Emerson was born in 1803 in Boston. His father, a minister, died when Emerson was eight. His mother managed to support the family so that Emerson and his brothers could go to school. Emerson studied at Harvard, and he too became a minister. He married shortly after beginning his Unitarian ministry, but his first wife died of tuberculosis less than 18 months later. He suffered many personal tragedies in his life including the death of his son, but he did not alter his optimistic approach to life.

After the death of his first wife, Emerson resigned from his ministerial post in Boston. He felt that he could no longer conduct some of the rituals which he felt come in the way of religious and spiritual experience. He wrote once that "I like the silent church before the service begins, better than any preaching" (1990, p. 162).

He then began a career as a writer and lecturer and earned his living through the lectures he gave all over the United States. Although not a dynamic speaker he spoke with such sincerity that James Russell Lowell wrote: "I have heard some great speakers and some accomplished orators, but never any that so moved and persuaded me as he" (cited in McAleer, 1984, p. 493).

One lecture that stands out was given at Harvard Divinity School in 1838. After this address it was to be 30 years before he was invited back to Harvard because his ideas were considered to be beyond the accepted views of the day. McAleer (1984) summarizes the address:

> In strictly theological terms, the basic message of the Divinity address was that man by responding intuitively through nature, to the moral sentiment expresses his divinity. Christ taught that "God incarnates himself in man." Christian leaders have failed their fellowman because they have neglected to explore "the Moral Nature . . . as the fountain of the established teaching in society." They have fossilized Christianity by putting too much emphasis on formal ritual. True faith is attained only when a man experiences a personal awareness of the Supreme Spirit dwelling within him. (p. 249)

With regard to education Emerson taught school as a young man. Howard Mumford Jones (1966) recounts his history as a teacher: "In 1821 he assisted his brother William in a girls' school in Roxbury, Massachusetts, where he was shy and awkward but managed to impress. In 1825 he taught at Chelmsford, in 1826 again at Roxbury, and a little later at Cambridge" (p. 2).

A resident of Concord most of his life, he was virtually a permanent member of the local school committee. Emerson was deeply loved by people in his community. When his house burned down, members of the community help rebuild his home while he was away in Europe. He died in 1882.

His view of education was closely connected to his overall philosophy which was holistic in nature. Emerson (1990) wrote: "Nothing is quite beautiful alone, nothing but is beautiful in the whole. A single

object is only so far beautiful as it suggests this universal grace"
(p. 26). Emerson saw elements in relation to one another almost in a
holographic sense:

> Each particle is a microcosm, and faithfully renders the likeness
> of the world . . . so intimate is this unity that, it is easily seen, it
> lies under the undermost garment of Nature and betrays it source
> in Universal Spirit. (p. 37)

Emerson (1990) rejects atomistic and fragmented approaches.
He felt that people were struggling with the problem of fragmentation
when he wrote: "The reason the world lacks unity, and lies broken
and in heaps, is because man is disunited with himself" (p. 54). To
address this problem Emerson wrote that the individual "should be
instructed that the inward is more valuable than their outward estate"
(p. 60). He also wrote: "In yourself is the law of all nature" (p. 99).
Emerson writes in the tradition of the great mystics as education
should awaken students to this law within.

With the emphasis now on testing in our schools, we can imagine
Emerson would not be pleased with the current educational priorities.
Instead, Emerson (1990) called for schools and colleges to inspire the
imagination of the young. He wrote:

> Colleges . . . can only highly serve us when they aim not to drill
> but to create; when they gather from far every ray of various
> genius to their hospitable halls, and, by the concentrated fires,
> set the hearts of their youth on flame. (p. 88)

By setting the "hearts of their youth on flame" students will discover their destinies. Emerson believed that "Each man has his own
calling. . . . There is one direction to every man in which unlimited
space is open to him . . . on that side all obstruction is taken away"
(p. 73). Education then should help people find their own destiny or
calling. How different this is from the career education that we hear
about today where people must find a job to compete in the global
economy.

Emerson's view of education is that it should nurture soul. The
individual for Emerson is a reflection of that universal spirit, or what
he calls the *Oversoul*. Education then should allow for contemplation
where the soul can witness from a more inclusive perspective:

We live on different planes or platforms. There is an external life, which is educated at school, taught to read, write, cipher and trade; taught to grasp all the boy can get, urging him to put himself forward, to make himself useful and agreeable in the world, to ride, run, argue and contend, unfold his talents, shine, conquer and possess. But the inner life sits at home, and does not learn to do things nor values these feats at all. 'Tis quiet, wise perception. It loves truth, because it is itself real; it loves right, it knows nothing else; but it makes no progress; was as wise in our first memory of it as now; is just the same now in maturity and hereafter in age, as it was in youth. We have grown to manhood and womanhood; we have powers, connection, children, reputations, professions: this makes no account of them all. It lives in the great present; it makes the present great. This tranquil, well founded, wide-seeing soul is no express-rider, no attorney, no magistrate: it lies in the sun and broods on the world. (Cited in Geldard, 1993, p. 172)

Education then should provide opportunities for contemplation such as being mindful as outlined in Chapter 6. Also just providing silent moments between classroom activities can also support a contemplative atmosphere.

More important than any technique is the teacher's awareness of nonverbal communication. Emerson (1990) wrote: "The action of the soul is oftener in that which is felt and left unsaid then that which is said in conversation" (p. 178). The teacher needs to be aware of his or her tone of voice and all the nonverbal messages that he or she sends to others. The presence of the teacher is central to Emerson's vision of education. He wrote: "The infallible index of true progress is the tone the man takes. . . . That which we are, we shall teach" (p. 182). More specifically he encouraged the teacher in this way:

By simple living, by an illimitable soul, you inspire, you correct, you instruct, you raise, you embellish all. By your own act you teach the beholder how to do the practicable. According to the depth from which you draw your life not only of your strenuous effort but of your manners and presence. (Cited in Jones, 1966, p. 227)

How can the teacher seek such depth and presence? Again contemplative living is the principal means. This means living more in the present and also living and teaching more spontaneously. Emerson (1990) stated: "For practical success, there must not be too much design. . . . All good conversation, manners and action, come from a spontaneity which forgets usages and makes the moment great. Nature hates calculators, her methods are salutatory and impulsive" (pp. 237–238).

Emerson's ideas are close to the notion of the "teachable moment." I believe the Emersonian teacher has a plan which is also flexible and open. Teachers should be open with their own feelings. Emerson (1990) once wrote in reference to a preacher but I think it also applies to the teacher:

> The preacher had lived in vain. He had not one word intimating that he had laughed or wept, was married or in love, had been commended, or cheated or chagrined. If he had ever lived and acted we were none the wiser for it. (p. 116)

At times teachers should not be afraid to reveal part of themselves and say something about their passions and interests. This allows that student to see the teacher as a human being and not just in the role of teacher.

Thoreau

Emerson was both mentor and friend to Thoreau, although their relationship cooled somewhat over the years. In conventional terms, Thoreau's life can be viewed as a failure since he held no job and unlike Emerson his writing was not well known during his lifetime. After his death, however, he has become a central figure in American letters and social history because of *Walden* and his nonviolent philosophy which influenced Tolstoy, Gandhi, and Martin Luther King.

Thoreau lived from 1817 to 1862 in Concord, Massachusetts. He studied at and graduated from Harvard in 1837. He said of his Harvard education that he was taught all the "branches of learning but none of the roots." He taught school briefly during his student days and after his graduation he took a teaching position in Concord at the Center School, which was a college preparatory school. Very early in his tenure there, one of his supervisors requested that Thoreau use corporal punishment on the students since he felt that the students were too noisy. Thoreau then applied the cane to six students the next day. He was so upset by what he did that he resigned that evening.

Not deterred by this experience Thoreau started his own school in 1838. The school, the Concord Academy, had only four students but he was able to continue for a year so that there were enough students to continue and to hire his brother, John, to help teach the additional students who had enrolled. The school was traditional in many ways as the students studied academic subjects both in the morning and afternoon. However, a significant feature of the school was the field activities. Sanborn (1917) describes one of these activities in his early biography of Thoreau:

> Henry Thoreau called attention to a spot on the rivershore, where he fancied the Indians had made their fires, and perhaps had a fishing village. . . . "Do you see," said Henry, "anything here that would be likely to attract Indians to this spot?" One boy said, "Why, here is the river for their fishing"; another pointed to the woodland near by, which could give them game. "Well, is there anything else?" pointing out a small rivulet that must come, he said, from a spring not far off, which could furnish water cooler than the river in the summer; and a hillside above it that would keep off the north and northwest wind in winter. Then, moving inland a little farther, and looking carefully about, he struck his spade several times, without result. Presently, when the boys began to think their young teacher and guide was mistaken, his spade struck a stone. Moving forward a foot or two, he set his space in again, stuck another stone, and began to dig in a circle. He soon uncovered the red, fire-marked stones of the long-disused Indian fireplace; thus proving that he had been right in his conjecture. Having settled the point, he carefully covered up his find and replaced the turf, not wishing to have the domestic altar of the aborigines profaned by mere curiosity. (pp. 205–206)

Thoreau was able to use these field experiences to foster inquiry and observation. "Wisdom," he wrote, "does not inspect, but behold" (cited in Bickman, 1999, p. 60). He felt that by observing things close at hand we can gain the greatest understanding. Thoreau wrote: "I wish so to live ever as to derive my satisfactions and inspirations from the commonest events, every-day phenomena, so that what my senses perceive, my daily walk, the conversation of my neighbors, may inspire me, and I may dream of no heaven but that which lies about me" (Bickman, p. 42). His descriptions of his experiences at Walden are evidence of his ability to draw so much from his daily observations. Contemplation, or more specifically awareness, was important to Thoreau. "No method nor discipline can supersede the necessity of being forever on the alert" (Thoreau, 1854/2004, p. 111). Thoreau believed in the value of direct experience. He once wrote in his journal: "We reason from our hands to our head" (Bickman, p. 51). He also felt that learning should be embodied and not confined to the head: "A man thinks as well through his legs and arms as his brain. We exaggerate the importance and exclusiveness of the headquarters" (Thoreau, 1906, Journal XIII: pp. 69–70).

Thoreau felt that writing and speaking should flow naturally and not be overly encumbered by concern for grammar:

> The first requisite and rule is that expression shall be vital and natural. . . . Essentially your truest poetic sentence is as free and lawless as a lamb's bleat. The grammarian is often one who can neither cry or laugh, yet thinks that he can express human emotions. (Journal XI: p. 386)

The field studies example cited above also demonstrates how Thoreau saw the role of teacher as guide and mutual inquirer. He said that he felt that "We should seek to be fellow students with the pupil, and should learn of, as well as with him, if we would be most helpful to him" (cited in Bickman, 1999). Thoreau was an advocate of continuous learning and adult education. This continuous learning was not a search for information but a deep connection to the cosmos through contemplation:

> My desire for knowledge is intermittent but my desire to commune with the spirit of the universe—to be intoxicated even with the fumes, call it, of that divine nectar—to bear my head through atmospheres and over heights unknown to my feet—is perennial & constant. (Journal III: p. 185)

Thoreau was a man who grounded his thinking in experience with the natural world, but like Emerson and Alcott, he was drawn to a higher vision.

Bronson Alcott

Alcott (1799–1888), a friend of both Emerson and Thoreau, devoted much of his life to education. The father of the writer, Louisa May Alcott, he struggled throughout his life to support his family and Emerson frequently came to his aid. In the 1840s Alcott helped found two cooperative communities—Brook Farm and Fruitlands. Fruitlands was a vegetarian community where the members even avoided wearing leather shoes. This community barely lasted a year and could not make it through the winter of 1844.

Alcott believed in the preexistence of the soul. He thus saw the child as coming into the world not as a tabula rasa but as charged with a divine mission. He wrote a manuscript entitled *Observations on the Spiritual Nurture of My Children* which was based on the idea that each child has a soul that needs to be nurtured and developed. He observed his children and their behavior and then speculated on the reasons for their behavior. For example, he wrote:

> Anna is apt to *theorize* both for herself and Louisa; whereas Louisa, intent solely on *practice,* is constantly demolishing Anna's ideal castles and irritating her Spirit with Gothic rudeness. The one builds; the other demolishes; and between the struggle of contrary forces, their tranquility is disturbed. . . . (Cited in Bedell, 1980, p. 83)

While Alcott lived in Philadelphia, he taught at the School of Human Culture where he tried to nurture the spiritual development of the children. Although his tenure at the school was short lived, letters and documents from the school inspired Alcott's friend, Elizabeth Peabody, to help him start a new school in Boston in 1834. Named the Temple School, this school has its place in the history of holistic education. It was called the Temple School because it was housed in the two rooms at the top of the Masonic Temple which was directly across from the Boston Commons. Elizabeth Peabody was instrumental to the work of the school. She helped recruit students, taught there, and also recorded many of the conversations that Alcott held with the students there. The school opened in September 1834, and 18 students were there the first day. The students were between the ages of 5 and 10 and came from some of the most famous families in Boston.

Alcott taught them both reading and writing simultaneously. He had them print the letters first before writing script "understanding—as no one had before him—that coordination between hand and eye in writing script was too difficult for young children to master " (Bedell, 1980, p. 94). In writing he wanted the students to express their thoughts and feelings and not just copy something from a book. In discussions Alcott also encouraged the students to stand up and speak out. One student stated: "I never knew I had a mind till I came to this school" (p. 96). Alcott did not use corporal punishment but instead used abandonment or the threats of abandonment.

By the winter the enrollment had doubled. Elizabeth Peabody, who had first contracted to work just 2 hours a day, now stayed for the entire school day and began to keep her record of the school. According to Bedell (1980), *The Record of a School* remains today probably the best exploration of Bronson Alcott's theories on education" (p. 102). Published in 1835, the book was part of larger movement of social change that included women's rights and anti-slavery activities. Bedell suggests that *The Record of a School* became a "symbol of a whole new era in American thought" (p. 103). Alcott himself had never been happier or felt more fulfilled; he wrote that he had found "a unity and a fullness" in his existence (p. 98).

The most unusual features of the school were the conversations that Alcott held with students regarding spiritual matters. Elizabeth Peabody wrote once that "Education depends on its attitude toward soul" (cited in Howell, 1991, p. xvii). Alice Howell writes how Alcott was able to incorporate this attitude into his teaching:

> That the child is not a *tabula rasa* Alcott proves without a doubt. As we read we rediscover that children are far more capable of philosophical insights and intuitions than we usually think, that indeed they take delight in being taken seriously as individuals whose opinions are worthy of respect. . . . (p. xxxii)

Below is an example of one of his conversations recorded by Elizabeth Peabody in her book *Record of a School: Exemplifying the General Principles of Spiritual Culture* (1836). This conversation of students took place after Alcott had read a passage from the Bible about John the Baptist in the desert. He asked the students: "What came to mind while I was reading?"

Josiah: The deserts seemed to me a great space with sand, like that in the hour-glass. The sun was shining on it, and making it sparkle. There were no trees. John was there alone.

Edward J: I thought the deserts mean woods, with paths here and there.

Lucy: I thought of a space covered with grass and some wild flowers, and John walking about.

Charles: I thought of a prairie.

Alexander: I thought of a few trees scattered over the country, with bees in the trunks.

George K: I thought of a place without houses, excepting John's; and flowers, trees and bee-hives.

(Bickman, Vol. 1, p. 61)

Martin Bickman (2004), who cites this passage, compares this discussion to creative visualization which was discussed in Chapters 4 and 6. Bickman also comments that Alcott lets the conversation go on without acting in the traditional role of being the central switchboard. Bickman acknowledges that sometimes Alcott could be manipulative in his teaching but mainly he tried to encourage students to find their own imagery and develop their own line of thinking. Bickman cites Dahlstrand (1982) to support his conclusion:

Alcott's paradigm gave the children a means of experiencing their minds. It served as structure on which they could build ideas. In one sense the paradigm limited them, but in another important way it freed them—it freed them from the tyranny of disorganization. In time they could cast away the paradigm, but the thought processes it helped them develop could stay with them forever. . . . Almost despite himself, his methods succeeded. (p. 127)

Another book about the school entitled *Conversations with Children on the Gospels* was edited by Alcott and published in 1836. This book received very negative reviews. One writer called Alcott "either insane or half-witted" while preachers felt that the conversations showed no respect for Christ's divinity. These attacks and debts during an economic recession led to the closing of the school.

Later in his career Emerson helped get Alcott hired as superintendent of schools for the Concord Schools. One of the projects he tried to undertake was to have Thoreau write a text on Concord's local history and geography. However, Thoreau died before the project could be completed.

Alcott, Emerson, and Thoreau identified many of the characteristics of timeless learning. They believed in the power of the individual *soul*. I believe that all three would echo Peabody's idea that "Education depends on its attitude toward soul." (Cited in Howell, p. xvii) Emerson (cited in Jones, 1966) also wrote: "the young child, the young man, requires no doubt rare patience: a patience that nothing but faith in the remedial forces of the soul can give" (p. 222).

They saw *contemplation* as a way to the deepest forms of learning. Closely linked with the idea of soul and contemplation was the *mysterious* nature of things. Emerson (cited in Jones, 1966) wrote: "Is not the Vast an element of the mind? Yet what teaching, what book of this day appeals to the Vast?" (p. 210).

Yet they also felt that learning should be *embodied*. Thoreau articulated this element of timeless learning most clearly as he wrote in his journal: "We reason from our hands to our head." Also he wrote: "The forcible writer stands bodily behind his words with his experience" (both cited in Bickman, 1999, p. 71). Alcott in the Temple School also developed an approach to learning that was *holistic*. Martin Bickman comments: "The education was what we would now call 'holistic,' since skills like spelling, grammar, and vocabulary were integrated into larger lessons on ethical and spiritual matters" (cited in Bickman, 1999, p. xxiii).

As noted in Chapter 2, Emerson suggested that timeless learning cannot be measured. This does not mean that teachers who focus on timeless learning are not accountable but we have to use different forms of assessment.

Finally, they all advocated a learning that was connected. The Thoreau example cited above shows how he connected learning to the environment. Emerson in his reference to the Vast suggested learning should be connected to the spiritual. Alcott felt that all teaching and learning should be connected to the spiritual center, the soul. Alice Howell (1991), in commenting on Alcott's teaching, states:

Alcott's secret, and I believe, his success consisted in his approach to children; he worked from his innermost center toward the same one he knew existed in each of them. A bond of trust, mutual respect, and affection was established at that level, so that the usual ego-to-ego tussle between teacher and student was avoided. (p. xxxii)

HOLISTIC EDUCATION

Holistic education is an approach aimed at teaching the whole person. Holistic educators reject educational approaches that limit learning solely to the intellect or that train students so that they can compete in a global economy. They believe that we must see the student as a complete human being which includes a mysterious, timeless quality (e.g., the soul). Holistic educators argue that schooling limited to preparing students to compete in a global economy is lacking in this respect.

Very much related to this desire to see the wholeness of the individual is the rejection of fragmented approach to learning. Generally, school curricula have broken knowledge into courses, units, and lessons that are often filled with unrelated factual material. There is often little effort made to connect the material within the course or between courses. Math and science are seen as totally separate and unrelated to history. In contrast, holistic education cultivates a *curriculum of connections*. Some of these connections include linking forms of thinking, connecting body and mind, integrating curricula, nurturing various forms of community, making connections to the earth and its processes, and finally connecting in some way to the student's soul (Miller, 1996/2001).

Holistic education seeks a relationship between the whole and the part. Marcus Aurelius (1997) wrote in his meditations:

I am part of a whole that is governed by nature; next, that I stand in some intimate connection with other kindred parts. For remembering this, inasmuch as I am a part, I shall be discontented with none of the things that are assigned to me out of the whole. (p. 77)

Holism has it roots in the thinking of the ancients and the vision of indigenous people as well. It is not New Age but can be linked to the perennial philosophy discussed in Chapter 2. In education linking the part to the whole can mean that we do not focus on teaching strategies without linking the strategies to our vision of realizing wholeness in the person and the community. We have often fixated on technique as a way to solve problems. Sometimes the technique has been teaching phonics as the sole approach to reading or on testing as the sole means of accountability. Reductionism to technique has left education without a larger, inspiring vision.

Another important aspect of holistic education is *inclusion*. It is inclusive in two ways. First, it rejects labeling and segregating of students. Second, it also encourages the use of a wide range of teaching and learning strategies to reach diverse student populations. One way of approaching this inclusive approach to learning is through the concepts of transmission, transaction, and transformation (Miller & Seller, 1985).

Transmission learning involves a one-way movement of information from teacher or text to student. There is little or no opportunity for reflection or inquiry. Teaching methods usually consist of lecture and drill.

Transaction learning is based on the assumption that students construct their own meaning and understandings. This is facilitated through inquiry learning and problem solving. Knowledge is viewed as more fluid and less fixed.

Transformation learning acknowledges the inner life of the student and seeks to nurture that inner life. Education is seen as process where the student can transform himself or herself in positive ways as well as the world he or she encounters.

Holistic education includes all three approaches. There are situations where short lectures are appropriate. However, each teacher and school needs to develop the appropriate relationship of all three forms. There is no one model of holistic education; each form should be organically connected to its context. Ideally, the teacher develops a *rhythm* in moving from one approach to another. Problems develop when the teacher gets locked into only one of the approaches which leads to a static classroom energy.

Holistic learning also focuses on *integration and connection*. As much as possible, holistic education seeks learning situations where the knowledge becomes part of the child's experience. This concept was described by Walt Whitman in his poem "The Child Went Forth" which was cited in Chapter 6. The holistic teacher seeks integration so that what the child encounters becomes part of him or her. Too often in school, knowledge is acquired for a test and quickly forgotten. Holistic learning is not satisfied with this approach.

Below, six types of connections are described that attempt to facilitate holistic learning. These connections include:

Linear thinking and intuition

Relationship between mind and body

Relationship among subjects

Relationship between self and community

Earth connections

Self connections

(Miller, 1996/2001)

Linear Thinking and Intuition

Holistic approaches to thinking attempt to link analytic thought with intuition. One approach that represents the attempt to link the two is the work of Graham Wallas (1926) who describes a four-step process. The first step is *preparation,* where the individual gathers information relevant to the problem or project. At the second stage, *incubation,* the individual relaxes and does not make an effort to work consciously on the problem. Instead, it is suggested that images realign themselves as the individual consciously attends to something else. In the *illumination* stage the solution will occur often spontaneously and unexpectedly. The fourth stage is *verification,* or revision, where the individual puts the idea into use and consciously works with the idea in a more detailed manner. The second and third stages, then, are intuitive, while the first and fourth stages are more analytical.

One vehicle for cultivating intuition is imagery, either spontaneous or guided, discussed in the Chapters 4 and 6. Another tool for enhancing intuition is the use of metaphor. Metaphor encourages students to make connections between things and processes that are normally unrelated; for example, a fuel system and a circulatory system. By making these connections students begin to discover underlying patterns and principles.

Relationship Between Mind and Body

Holistic education attempts to connect mind and body. This process can begin with movement education for younger children.

Movement Education

Holistic education supports movement in the classroom. Dimondstein (1971) has developed a holistic approach to dance for the elementary school classroom. The focus of her approach is on developing kinesthetic awareness. Kinesthetic awareness refers to children's ability to control their movements and to feel the movements at the same time. With gestures they learn to give shape and form to their inner thoughts. Dance, then, is not just acting out inner feelings, but giving form to them through visual images expressed through movement. For example, in exploring the concept of fear, the children find some movement to express their conception of fear. The students can first start with unstructured visualization where they let images of fear come into their minds. They can articulate these images or draw them, and finally they can express their image through movement.

Yoga and other disciplines can also be used to facilitate body-mind connections. Rachel Carr (1977) suggests that yoga for younger children can focus on students being like animals. In the *cobra* pose the student can be like a snake as the child arches the back. In doing the *locust* the children become like insects as their legs are arched high like a grasshopper.

Subject Connections

Curriculum Integration

The term *subject connections* refers to how we can link and integrate subjects so that they are relevant to the concerns of students. James Beane (1997) has written on this subject and developed a powerful model for integration based around the questions that arise from students. In planning for integration he suggests that the teacher solicit questions from students under two categories: self and world. He suggests that students be put in small groups and that they develop responses to the questions: "What questions or concerns do you have about yourself?" and "What questions or concerns do you have about the world?" (p. 51). Examples of these questions include:

Self Questions

How long will I live?

What will I look like when I am older?

Do other people think I am the way I think I am?

What job will I have?

Will I get married and have children?

World Questions

Will we ever live in outer space?

Why are there so many crimes?

Will racism ever end?

Will the rain forests be saved?

Why are there so many poor people?

After looking at these questions the students then develop lists of sample themes. A few themes suggested in Beane (1997) included:

jobs, money, careers

environmental problems

drugs, diseases, health

"isms" and prejudice (pp. 51–52)

The students then vote to decide which theme they want to pursue. The strength of this model is that it is a bottom-up strategy that builds on student concerns.

Community Connections

Holistic education seeks to develop community within classrooms and schools and also connect students to the community that surrounds the schools. Finally, holistic education seeks to connect the student to the global community as well.

In the classroom the teacher attempts to create an atmosphere of trust that supports the development of community. This is done through conveying respect for students, listening attentively, and being genuine in conveying one's feelings. Mindfulness discussed in the last chapter is one of the principal means of doing this.

Community can also be fostered through cooperative learning. In cooperative learning students work in small groups on various tasks. There is evidence that cooperative learning facilitates the student's social, emotional, and intellectual development (Slavin, 1994).

Students can be connected to community through service learning. Service learning engages the student in community activity. These activities can include helping at a day care center or nursing home, cleaning up a park, or protesting industrial pollution. In service learning the student should not just conduct the activity but also have an opportunity to reflect on the activity back in school. Service learning is described in more detail in Chapter 5.

Finally, holistic education and global education are closely linked. It is important for students to see themselves as global citizens. Robert Muller's (n.d.) concept of a world core curriculum is relevant, as certain concepts, principles, and values are essential to the planet's survival. Muller suggests that schools throughout the world should focus on fundamental, universal themes that help students to see themselves as part of a global family. There are schools that are basing their curriculum on Muller's ideas of a world core curriculum.

Earth Connections

Environmental education has become part of the school curriculum. Unfortunately, in many cases it has focused on a problem-solving approach to the environment where we can fix things through recycling or other technical solutions. What is needed is an environmental education that centers on a sense of the sacred and how we are deeply embedded in the natural processes of the earth. Some examples of this have already been given in Chapter 5 which described examples of how children can care for plants and trees.

Self Connections

This connection refers not to our ego but our big self. In his novel *Rabbit at Rest,* John Updike (1990) describes how Rabbit toward the end of his life turns inward and connects with his heart and a sort of inner magic, which he occasionally experiences as a "feeling of collaboration or being bigger than he really is."

Literature, mythology, and story allow the Self to emerge. Children's literature can be a conveyor of wisdom and wonder. Fairy tales, myths, and all forms of children's literature from around the world can help nourish the child's Self. In Africa, for example, the young child is seen as a messenger from the other world.

Science can nurture Self. Brian Swimme and Thomas Berry (1992) make a powerful case for studying what they call the *Universe Story* from the big bang to the present moment. This story allows the student to awaken to the wonder of existence:

> Earth seems to be a reality that is developing with the simple aim of celebrating the joy of existence. This can be seen in the coloration of the various plants and animals, in the circling flights of the swallows, as well as the blossoming of the springtime flowers, each of these events required immense creativity over billions of years in order to come forth as Earth. Only now do we begin to understand that this story of the Earth is also the story of the human, as well as the story of every being of the Earth. . . . The final benefit of this story might be to enable the human community to present to the larger Earth community in a mutually enhancing manner. (p. 3)

Swimme and Berry suggest that we are moving from a technological age—the *Technozoic* era—to an ecological era—the *Ecozoic* era. They call for a United Species that would transcend the United Nations. This new organization could be based on the World Charter for Nature passed by the United Nations Assembly in 1982.

Although the Universe Story is based on the observations of science, it also includes the humanities. Swimme and Berry argue that literature, myth, poetry, music, and all the arts can also express much of the mystery and wonder associated with the story of the universe. Besides the book by Swimme and Berry, there are also videos that can be used in classrooms to help students engage the Universe Story. In sum, the Universe Story could provide a powerful organizing theme for the whole curriculum.

Like most forms of timeless learning holistic education depends on the presence of the teacher. The holistic teacher should be working toward making connections both personally and in the classroom. Guidelines for doing this will be explored more fully in Chapter 9.

SLOW EDUCATION

Slow education is connected to the slow food movement that arose in Italy in the 1980s. In 1986, when a McDonald's franchise opened in Rome, a journalist asked why there could not be "slow food" in addition to fast food. The idea caught on and now there is an International Slow Food Congress which meets every year. There is now even a "slow city" in Italy which in its founding manifesto declared: "A firm defense of quiet material pleasure is the only way to oppose the universal folly of Fast Life" (cited in Holt, 2002, p. 266).

Like holistic education, slow education is opposed to the mechanical product orientation of standards-led school reform. Maurice Holt (2002) suggests that the accountability movement creates "a system of schools geared solely to the product—test results—and not to the process of creating educative experiences (cited in Holt, p. 268)" Holt concludes: "The result of creating fast schools is institutional indigestion, and signs of discomfort are now appearing" where "courses crammed in too much material at the expense of understanding" (p. 268).

In contrast, slow education encourages students to pursue questions in depth and not skip quickly through a curriculum of unrelated facts. Holt (2002) suggests that:

> one takes time to see what Newton's concepts of mass and force might imply, to appreciate their abstract nature and the intellectual leap they represent. Then the usual algorithms fall into place quickly and securely. The slow school offers the intellectual space for scrutiny, argument and resolution. (p. 269)

Holt suggests that the increase of homeschooled children is also a form of slow education as parents want children to have a more flexible approach to learning. When our approach to teaching and learning slows down, then students can actually have moments where time stops and they experience timeless learning. Many spiritual teachers have encouraged the spiritual practitioner to slow down. Eknath Easwaran (1989) has written about what he calls "hurry sickness" in our society that can be met through patience and slowing down. David Elkind (1989) wrote about the "hurried child" whose day is constantly crammed with planned activities. He calls for a more relaxed childhood that is congruent with the slow school movement.

Carl Honore (2004) has also discussed slow education in his book *In Praise of Slowness*. He describes how the former dean of undergraduate education at Harvard, Harry Lewis, sent a letter to all incoming students that was entitled *Slow Down*. In the letter Lewis encouraged students to get more out of their education by doing less.

CONCLUSION

Slow education does not have an explicit spiritual dimension. Holistic education can be practiced in this manner as the most of the connections are not overtly spiritual. However, the line is sometimes fine between what is spiritual and what is not. For example, in caring for trees or plants a sense of reverence can arise in the students. Some would call this spiritual. Timeless learning certainly does not draw a line in the sand between what is spiritual and what is not since this is counter to the underlying perspective of interconnectedness. Perhaps Wittgenstein's admonition of "whereof what we cannot speak let us be silent" can be followed; we can acknowledge the difficulty in conceptualizing and talking about spirituality.

REFERENCES

Alcott, A. B. (1836–1837). *Conversations with children on the gospels; conducted and edited by A. Bronson Alcott.* Boston: J. Munroe.

Aurelius, M. (1997). *Meditations* (W. Kaufmann, Ed.). Mineola, NY: Dover.

Beane, J. (1997). *Curriculum integration: Designing the core of democratic education.* New York: Teachers College Press.

Bedell, M. (1980). *The Alcotts: Biography of a family.* New York: Crown.

Bickman, M. (Ed.). (1999). *Uncommon learning: Henry David Thoreau on education.* Boston: Houghton Mifflin.

Bickman, M. (2004). *Minding American education: Reclaiming the tradition of active learning.* New York: Teachers College Press.

Buell, L. (1973). *Literary transcendentalism: Style and vision in the American renaissance.* Ithaca, NY: Cornell University Press.

Carr, R. (1977). *Be a frog, bird or a tree.* New York: Harper Colophon.

Cromphout, G. V. (2003). Emerson in the twenty-first century. *The Concord Saunterer, 11,* 7–8.

Dahlstrand, F. C. (1982). *Amos Bronson Alcott: An intellectual biography.* East Brunswick, NJ: Associated University Press.

Dimondstein, G. (1971). *Children dance in the classroom.* New York: Macmillan.

Easwaran, E. (1989). *Original goodness: Strategies for uncovering hidden spiritual resources.* Berkeley, CA: Nilgiri Press.

Elkind, D. (1989). *The hurried child.* Reading, MA: Addison Wesley.

Emerson, R. W. (1990). *Selected essays, lectures and poems* (R. Richardson, Ed.). New York: Bantam.

Emerson, R. W. (1996). *Hitch your wagon to a star and other quotations from Ralph Waldo Emerson* (K. Frome, Ed.). New York: Columbia University Press.

Geldard, R. (1993). *The esoteric Emerson: The spiritual teachings of Ralph Waldo Emerson.* Hudson, NY: Lindisfarne.

Harding, W., & Bode, C. (Eds.). (1974). *Correspondence of Henry Thoreau.* Westport, CT: Greenwood.

Holt, M. (2002). It's time to start the slow school movement. *Phi Delta Kappan, 84*(4), 265–271.

Honore, C. (2004). *In praise of slowness: How a worldwide movement is challenging the cult of speed.* San Francisco: Harper.

Howell, A. O. (1991). Education and the soul of the child. In A. B. Alcott, *How like an angel came I down* (A. Howell, Ed.). Hudson, NY: Lindisfarne.

Jones, H. M. (Ed.). (1966). *Emerson on education: Selections.* New York: Teachers College Press.

McAleer, J. (1984). *Ralph Waldo Emerson: Days of encounter.* Boston: Little, Brown.

Miller, J. (1996/2001). *The holistic curriculum.* Toronto: OISE Press.

Miller, J. (2000). *Education and the soul: Toward a spiritual curriculum.* Albany: SUNY Press.

Miller, J., & Seller, W. (1985). *Curriculum: Perspectives and practice.* New York: Longman.

Muller, R. (n.d.). A world core curriculum for global education. Retrieved March 18, 2005, from http://www.unol.org/rms/wcc.html

Peabody, E. P. (1836). *Record of a school: Exemplifying the general principles of spiritual culture* (2nd ed.). Boston: Russell Shattuck.

Sanborn, F. B. (1917). *The life of Henry David Thoreau.* Boston: Houghton Mifflin.

Slavin, R. (1994). *Cooperative learning: Theory, research and practice.* Boston: Allyn & Bacon.

Swimme, B., & Berry, T. (1992). *The universe story: From the primordial flaring forth to the ecozoic era—A celebration of the unfolding of the cosmos.* San Francisco: Harper.

Thoreau, H. D. (1906). *The journals of Henry David Thoreau* (Vols. 1–14) (B. Torrey & F. H. Allen, Eds.). Boston: Houghton Mifflin.

Thoreau, H. D. (1981–2002). *The writings of Henry David Thoreau: Journal* (Vols. 1–8) (Witherell, E. H., Editor-in-Chief). Princeton, NJ: Princeton University Press. (Original work published 1906)

Thoreau, H. D. (2004). *Walden* (L. D. Shanley, Ed.). Princeton, NJ: Princeton University Press. (Original work published 1854)

Updike, J. (1990). *Rabbit at rest.* New York: Knopf.

Wallas, G. (1926). *The art of thought.* London: Watts.

CHAPTER EIGHT

Examples of Timeless Learning

Only a man who lives not in time but in the present is happy.

—Wittgenstein

The teacher who lives in the present is able to create the classroom that children want to be in. There are schools that explicitly nurture timeless learning; these include the Krishnamurti schools, Montessori education, and Waldorf education. Although challenging in today's climate of high stakes testing, timeless learning can also be practiced in public schools—how teachers can do this is explored in the next chapter.

KRISHNAMURTI SCHOOLS

Surely a life that has significance, the riches of true happiness, is not of time. Like love, such a life is timeless; and to understand that which is timeless we must not approach it through time but to understand time.

—Krishnamurti, 1996, p. 80

One professor called Krishnamurti's life timeless (Buultjens, 1996, p. vii). Krishnamurti spent most of his life traveling around the world speaking to groups. He was identified as the World Teacher by the Theosophical Society when Charles Leadbeater, one of the society's leaders, saw him as a young boy in India. He was then raised in England by Annie Besant, another one of the society's leaders. However, he left the society in late 1929 when he said "truth was a pathless land and you cannot approach it by any path whatsoever, by any religion, by any sect" (cited in Blau, 1995, p. 85). Krishnamurti, who died in 1986, was very interested in education and he founded several schools. These include five schools in India, one in England, and one in California. Since his death in 1986 two more schools based on his ideas have been founded in India.

Krishnamurti's ideas about education are presented in several books (1953, 1974, 1978). For Krishnamurti (1953) the aim of education is to "bring about an integrated individual who is capable of dealing with life as a whole" (p. 24). This ability to see life as a whole involves what Krishnamurti calls intelligence. In his words, "Intelligence is the capacity to perceive the essential *what is;* and to awaken this capacity, in oneself and in others, is education" (p. 14). Perceiving *what is* means not being caught up in ideals or models that get in the way of being in the present moment. This idea of being present to *what is* relates to timeless learning. In a paper on "Time and Transformation" Krishnamurti (1996) writes:

> When you no longer depend on time as a means of transforming *what is* because you see the falseness of that process, then you are confronted with *what is,* and you are interested to understand *what is,* naturally you have a quiet mind. . . . Thus regeneration is only possible in the present, not in the future, not tomorrow. (pp. 82–83)

Education then for Krishnamurti should bring students and teachers into the present, or the timeless moment. Being present in the moment allows the person to be free where the individual is no longer confined by cultural conditioning. In Krishnamurti's words:

> Education in the true sense is helping the individual to be mature and free, to flower greatly in love and goodness. That is what we should be interested in, and not in shaping the child according to some idealistic pattern. (1953, p. 23)

Self-knowledge, or "awareness of one's total psychological process" was another important aim for Krishnamurti. He believed that the student should "observe and understand his own self-projected values" and the conditioning influences that have influenced the student. Students learn to see themselves clearly and their relationship to others and the surrounding environment.

Closely related to development of intelligence and self-knowledge is the realization of wisdom. For Krishnamurti (1953), "Wisdom comes from the abnegation of self" (p. 64). When we are rooted in competition and greed, the self dominates. When we let go of the notion of me and mine and abide in a love, wisdom arises naturally. Krishnamurti spoke frequently of the importance of love and compassion as he felt love and intelligence are closely connected. He stated "to understand our responsibility, there must be love in our hearts, not mere learning and knowledge" (p. 78). Finally, Krishnamurti felt that education should help shape a new set of values. It should not just reinforce conformity and competition that exist in society but help in the transformation to where freedom, creativity, and peace are more deeply respected and experienced in daily life.

Principles of Learning

How can these goals be achieved? First, we have to give up the educator's obsession with technique. Krishnamurti (1953) stated: "Present-day education is a complete failure because it has over-emphasized technique. In over-emphasizing technique we destroy man" (p. 18). His words still apply today, perhaps even more so. The present-day obsession with accountability and standards is just another form of deadening technique. Of course, educators must be accountable, but the almost pathological emphasis on comparing test scores between individuals, schools, and countries is actually interfering with the learning process. School has become a game where the emphasis is on teaching to the test. In the present environment fear tends to predominate rather than risk-taking which is one of the most important elements in significant learning.

Educational reform has also tended to emphasize technique with regard to curriculum and instruction. Unfortunately, even holistic educators can fall into this trap and advocate a particular technique such as cooperative learning without linking the teaching technique to a larger context of holism. It should be noted that Krishnamurti felt that education should offer information and technical training but within the context of what he calls an "integrated outlook."

Krishnamurti was also critical of attempts to control children and to use rewards and punishments. The reason for this is straightforward, as how can the student become truly free, if he or she has to function in an environment of compulsion? Instead of discipline and compulsion, there should be an atmosphere of mutual affection and respect. This sense of respect must start with the teacher's respect for the student which the student must sense and feel in the classroom. Mutual respect arises in atmosphere where there is no fear. In Krishnamurti's words:

> The right kind of education must take into consideration this question of fear, because fear warps our whole outlook on life. To be without fear is the beginning of wisdom, and only the right kind of education can bring about the freedom from fear in which alone there is deep and creative intelligence. (1953, p. 34)

When rewards and punishments are used, they undermine the development of intelligence. In an environment of rewards and punishments, education becomes a game where students try to please the teacher. Krishnamurti pointed out that an education built on punishment and rewards supports a "social structure which is competitive, antagonistic and ruthless" (p. 35).

Alfie Kohn (1993) has summarized research in this area and his findings support Krishnamurti's insight. His research indicates that rewards and punishments, including grades, actually interfere with student learning. In short, the student learns more in an environment where there is not an emphasis on rewards and punishments. For example, Kohn cites several studies where students who were not rewarded with money or candy did better on tasks than those who were rewarded (p. 43). This finding held true for elementary school children as well university students. For example, in one study of high school students some students were rewarded for tasks related to memory and creativity and some were not. The students who were not rewarded performed significantly better on the tasks. Kohn concludes that when rewards are used extensively, students tend to be less creative in their work (p. 47).

Krishnamurti felt that traditional religious education was problematic because it was based on fear and rewards. It also discouraged inquiry into the nature of things which is at the heart of true education. At one point he stated:

True religious education is to help the child to be intelligently aware, to discern for himself the temporary and the real, and to have a disinterested approach to life; and would it not have more meaning to begin each day at home or at school with a serious thought, or with a reading that has depth and significance rather than mumble some oft-repeated words or phrases? (1953, p. 40)

Krishnamurti's vision of education is different than that of Rudolf Steiner who does recommend that the day begin with oft-repeated words and phrases. Although I believe that Steiner and Krishnamurti shared the same aims for education—that is the development of the free and integrated person, their approaches to pedagogy were quite different. As we shall see in the section on Steiner, he outlined a very detailed curriculum for every stage of the child's development. Krishnamurti did not; instead, he developed certain general principles for educators to follow. While Steiner had specific prescriptions for almost every aspect of life, Krishnamurti avoided such prescriptions because he felt it might result in some kind of inflexible dogma that undermines the freedom of the individual.

The Teacher

The task of the teacher is first to wake up and be aware of his or her own thoughts and feelings. Teachers should examine their own conditioning and its influences on their behavior.

I think another word that we could use here, even though Krishnamurti did not use the term, is "mindfulness" which was discussed in Chapter 6. Krishnamurti (1974) often talked about the importance of attention:

When you pay attention, you see things much more clearly. You hear the bird singing much more distinctly. You differentiate between various sounds. When you look at a tree with a great deal of attention, you see the whole beauty of the tree. You see leaves, the branch, you see the wind playing with it. When you pay attention, you see extraordinarily clearly. . . . Attention is very important, in the class, as well as when you are outside, when you are eating, when you are walking. Attention is an extraordinary thing. (p. 16)

For Krishnamurti the teacher should also be open and vulnerable. Vulnerability does not mean that teachers should continually be self-disclosing. It means, however, that when it seems appropriate teachers can share something of themselves. Below is a good example of this process by Rachael Kessler (1991):

> One night during my first year of teaching there was a blazing fire in my community, the roads were closed, and I was unable to get home to my family. I was able to contact them and know that they were safe, but I spent the night in town and came in to teach that morning. I felt so disconnected, worried, confused, and disoriented that I knew I couldn't be present without telling my students about the fire. I started the class by asking for their help: "You kids have all grown up here in California with fires, floods, earthquakes. This is new to me. How have you coped with disasters in your life?" This class was a turning point for that group. Previously reticent about their personal lives and feelings they jumped into this one with gusto. My authentic need, my vulnerability and a very hot topic had brought them to life. (p. 13)

At appropriate moments teachers can open themselves to their students. In these moments students begin to see us as human beings and not just as "teacher."

Krishnamurti also refers to spontaneity as an important element in teaching. He states "Intelligence is the spontaneous perception which makes a man strong and free" (1953, p. 103). Ideally there should be a balance between planned action and the spontaneous.

The student's inner life thrives in a climate where spontaneity is present and it withers in an environment which is overplanned and controlled. In education we give room for the spontaneous when we talk of the teachable moment. In the teachable moment the teacher moves away from the lesson plan and follows his or her intuition in working with the students. Kessler exploring her feelings about the fire was a good example of the teachable moment. The teachable moment is another form of timeless learning.

Krishnamurti believed that teaching is not just a job but a way of life. In some way the teacher should feel called to the profession. The teacher feels deep satisfaction in being with children and in assisting in their growth and development. Krishnamurti (1953) comments at one point: "One teaches because one wants the child to be rich inwardly" (p. 113). This statement is still significant today, as holistic education should address the inner life of the child. This can be done through the sensitivity of the teacher, the arts, fostering a connection to the earth, and using approaches such as meditation and visualization which actively nourish the inner life. I have developed these themes in other contexts (Miller, 1996, 2000).

Finally, Krishnamurti stated (1953) that "truth comes into being when there is a complete cessation. . . . When the mind is utterly still . . . it is silent, . . . then there is creation" (p. 125).

As mentioned earlier there are a few schools that have been founded on the principles described above. Below is a brief description of three of these schools.

The School

Krishnamurti argued that schools should be small. Large institutions by their very nature cannot be responsive to the needs of children. Again his insights are supported by the research. This research indicates that in small schools students participate more in the life of the school and that students in small schools actually do better academically (Cotton, 1996; Lee & Smith, 1994; Wasley, 2000). Despite this research, schools districts in North America over the past 20 years have tended to close small community-based schools and build larger institutions because they are supposedly more cost efficient. Yet there is also research that indicates that small schools can educate children at a lower cost (Sher, 1977). For example, in Vermont it was found that 6 of the top 10 schools in percentage of graduates entering college were small schools (fewer than 60 in the graduating class) and that they were able to produce these results with operating costs, on a per pupil basis, of $225 less than the large schools.

Krishnamurti also felt the classes should be small. There has been recognition of this fact by some educational reformers and as smaller class sizes have been mandated in various North America jurisdictions (e.g., California) particularly at the primary level.

Another element that Krishnamurti felt was important was a committed staff. He argued that teachers should be enthusiastic in their work and care deeply about the students in the school. The staff should also work together as a whole, which again is easier to do in a small school.

Krishnamurti suggested that teachers meet often as a whole group to make decisions. Decisions should not be made arbitrarily by the principal but by group consensus. The whole life of the teacher should also be addressed. If the teacher is having difficulties at home, Krishnamurti suggested that these problems can be discussed at the group meetings so that some form of support can be provided to the teacher. Krishnamurti was sensitive to the problems of teachers and stated that no teacher should be overburdened since this will adversely affect the teacher's work.

He also suggested that students be involved in school governance. Krishnamurti argued that student councils be formed that included both teachers and students and that dealt with problems such as discipline, cleanliness, and food. Students should actually supervise each other in these matters and thus learn self-government.

The Rajghat Besant School

This school in Varanasi, India, is a residential coeducational school with about 350 students ranging in age from 6 to 18. The students reside in 12 different houses. There are about 50 teachers and half of them live in the houses as House Parents. Besides the academic program there are also extracurricular activities including sports, yoga, gymnastics, art, music, dance, gardening, and working with computers. The aims of the school include:

- To help cultivate all aspects of the child—physical, intellectual, emotional, and aesthetic with a holistic development of all the faculties.
- To motivate children without punishment or reward and without encouraging competition.
- Not to condition the mind of the child in any belief, whether religious, social, or cultural.
- To encourage inquiry with an open mind, and a respect for dissent.
- To inculcate a love of Nature and a respect for all life.

Exams are not used in Grades 2 to 7; however, they are given in the higher grades because they are required for admission to university.

Brockwood Park School

This secondary school which is about an hour's drive from London, England, has approximately 60 students aged 13 to 20. The classes are very small and the teacher-student ratio is about 1:5. There is a strong aesthetic flavor to the school which is housed in a beautiful large building on 36 acres. Matthew Barnett (1999) reports that "painting, pottery, music and dance are strong and an aura of creative excitement permeates every corridor and classroom" (p. 36). Recently a new junior school, Inwoods, has been established on the grounds for young children aged 3 to 6. Most of the graduates from the Brockwood Park School continue on to university or some form of postsecondary education. The goals of the school include:

- To educate the whole human being.
- To explore what freedom and responsibility are in relationship with others and in modern society.
- To see the possibility of being free from self-centered action and inner conflict.
- To discover one's own talent and what right livelihood means.
- To learn the proper care, use, and exercise of the body.
- To appreciate the natural world, seeing our place in it and responsibility for it.
- To find the clarity that may come from having a sense of order and valuing silence.

Oak Park School

This school is located in Ojai, California, about 90 miles north of Los Angeles. The campus includes 150 acres, a main building, and an arts building. The school serves students from ages 3 to 18. There is a preschool that focuses on children's play. It nurtures the student's social and emotional development through art, storytelling, movement, and outdoor activities. In the elementary school, the student studies traditional subjects such as math, science, language arts, and social studies as well as a number of other subjects such as art, music, drama, play production, horticulture and cooking, computers, woodworking, library skills, and physical education. Classes are small with approximately 15 students in each class.

The junior high and high school offer a balanced approach to learning. There is emphasis on traditional subjects such as English, math, science, social studies, and foreign languages as well as an opportunity to reflect on oneself and one's relationship to others. In the junior high there is an integrated approach to learning as well as an opportunity to travel to Mexico and the American Southwest. In the high school, students study traditional subjects as well as psychology, philosophy, culture, and interpersonal relations. The focus generally is on inquiry and an investigative approach to learning.

Conclusion

All the Krishnamurti schools have small classes and strive to integrate academic learning into a broader, more holistic framework. All the schools emphasize the opportunity for student inquiry into important issues—both personal and social.

Roland Vernon (2000) in his biography of Krishnamurti has given an assessment of the schools. He writes: "If a school is to be judged by the rounded, open and positive outlook of its student leavers, together with their genuine affection for the staff and institution, the Krishnamurti schools must be said to have succeeded" (p. 263).

However, Vernon (2000) notes there is also a downside to the schools. Like other private schools, there can be a sense of elitism and alienation from the outside world. He also notes that the discouragement of competition particularly in sports can be a problem since it "removes zest from school life that a number of children do find natural and stimulating" (p. 264).

Krishnamurti's emphasis on being present to *what is* provides the basis for timeless learning. He keeps reminding us of the importance of approaching teaching and life itself with attention and not letting our minds become clouded with too many thoughts that prevent us from living in the present moment.

WALDORF EDUCATION

Rudolf Steiner, the founder of Waldorf education, was born in 1861 in a small town in the Austro-Hungarian Empire. He was a bright and inquisitive boy who was able to support himself from the age of 14 to 30 by tutoring. One boy whom he tutored was a hydrocephalic child who was mentally challenged and whose health was very fragile. Because the boy tired so easily, Steiner prepared his lessons very carefully so that learning could be done in a short period of time. The boy gradually became healthy and eventually entered the medical profession. Steiner felt that he learned a great deal about the learning process from this experience, and these understandings eventually led to Waldorf education.

At age 30 he edited the scientific writings of Goethe, who had a powerful impact on Steiner's thinking. Steiner investigated and developed approaches to many areas of human endeavor such as farming, architecture, and medicine. After World War I, he was asked to start a school based on an educational approach that might avoid the militaristic thinking that led to the war. The school was for the employees of the Waldorf cigarette factory in Stuttgart. Germany. The Waldorf movement, which began in 1919, has become one of the fastest growing independent school movements in the world.

Steiner's View of Development

Steiner based his pedagogy on his conception of the human being and it is important to briefly examine this conception of human development. Steiner sees the person as having four bodies, or sheaths, and that it is appropriate to emphasize each of these bodies at a different time in the child's education.

The first of these bodies is the *physical* body. It is this body which is dominant during the first seven years of life. The physical environment is very important for the child at this age. It needs to be rich in shape and color and also should offer behaviors which the child can physically imitate. The physical objects should be ones that children can work with and to which they can apply their imagination. For example, Steiner recommends that the child make a doll out of a napkin; most dolls do not have faces so the child can imagine the face that is appropriate. Singing and movement are also very important at this stage of development. The children will clap out numbers, and dance movements are seen to have strong influence on developing the physical organism.

The second body, the *etheric,* becomes predominant around age seven when children lose their baby teeth. According to Steiner (1975), "The etheric body is a force-form; it consists of active forces, and not of matter" (pp. 13–14). Education during the elementary school years is based on imagination and not the intellect. Steiner stressed that "it is not abstract ideas that have an influence on the developing etheric body, but living pictures that are seen and comprehended inwardly" (p. 32). Steiner concludes:

> The etheric body is worked upon through pictures and examples—i.e. by carefully guiding the imagination of the child. As before the age of seven we have to give the child the actual physical pattern for him to copy, so between the time of the change of teeth and puberty, we must bring into his environment things with the right inner meaning and value. For it is from the inner meaning and value of things that the growing child will now take guidance. Whatever is fraught with a deep meaning that works through pictures and allegories, is the right thing for these years. The etheric body will unfold its forces if the well-ordered imagination is allowed to take guidance from the inner meaning it discovers for itself in pictures and allegories—whether seen in real life or communicated to the mind. It is not abstract conceptions that work in the right way on the growing etheric body, but rather what is seen and perceived—not indeed with the outward senses, but with the eye of the mind. This seeing and perceiving is the right means of education for these years. (pp. 29–30)

In the elementary school years Waldorf emphasizes fairy tales, myth, and fables to stimulate the child's imagination. The child should not be rushed into intellectual activity; mental activity should be complemented with activities such as handwork where the students knit their own seat cushions or hats. Writing should be viewed as an imaginative manual activity and children should have the opportunity to write and tell stories aloud. Children should also have direct experiences with nature and objects instead of becoming too dependent on the written word.

Music is also very important during the elementary years. Music for Steiner (1975) "must bring to the etheric body that rhythm which will then enable it to sense in all things the rhythm otherwise concealed" (p. 42). Other arts such as drawing and drama are important and are often integrated with the main lesson which begins each day in a Waldorf school.

Games and gymnastic exercises are important at this level. Steiner suggested that these exercises must be thought out very carefully so that the etheric body is strengthened within the child. A certain approach to gymnastics called Bothmer was developed from Steiner's work by a Count Bothmer. Gymnastics, art, music, storytelling, and drama are all designed to nourish the child's soul which Richards (1980) claims is the central task of Steiner education (p. 59).

The third member of the human being is the *sentient* or *astral* body which is "the vehicle of pain and pleasure, of impulse, craving, passion, and the like—all of which are absent in a creature consisting only of physical and etheric bodies" (Steiner, 1975, p. 12). The astral body is predominant during adolescence. During this phase Waldorf education focuses more on developing the student's critical intelligence. The artistic element is kept but is woven into secondary school subjects with an emphasis on developing intellectual autonomy.

The fourth and final member of the human being is the human *ego*. Steiner's conception of the ego is really closer to the Self or soul, as Steiner says the "I" or the "God" begins to speak to the person from within when the fourth member begins to predominate.

Rhythm

Time is viewed rhythmically in Waldorf education. The flow of the seasons and the flow of the breath provide touch points, or metaphors, for the Waldorf teacher. Harwood (1958) comments:

All rhythm—not only that of the heart and lungs—is intimately involved with a process of breathing in and out. Every day is a time of the inbreathing of new experiences: every night a time of surrendering in sleep what has been won for good or ill during the day. Every year brings the contracting process of winter, when life sinks into the depths of the earth; and the expansiveness of the summer, when it soars with pollen into the far spaces of the atmosphere. Human life itself swings from the inbreathing of childhood and youth to the outbreathing of old age; it is bounded by the inbreath at birth which brings the first experience of the earth and the outbreath at death which carries the departing spirit into other worlds. (p. 73)

This rhythmic view of life and learning has a timeless quality as it is removed from chronological time.

Central to Waldorf education is eurythmy, Steiner's approach to movement. Eurythmy is used at all levels of Waldorf education, although it is probably most important during the elementary years because it is primarily related to activity of the etheric body. Eurythmy is not dance movement or personal expression; instead, it is a physical form of speech. The physical gestures are taken from the movements of the larynx. The arms and hands are very important in eurythmy. Eurythmy can also be performed to music and this is called "tone eurythmy."

In the early grades the children walk and run to form geometrical forms such as circles, figure eights, squares, triangles, and pentagons. Eurythmy can help the asocial child learn how to move in time with the other children, and can help the intellectual child to step in time to rhythm. Eurythmy can also be combined with storytelling at the primary grades. Harwood (1958) comments:

> If we are going to perform a little story in this sort of eurythmic action, music must also come in. The children begin to feel the qualities of different rhythms—perhaps the light anapest for the prince's horse galloping through the forest—the trochee for the princess lost at night in that same forest and thinking of the home she will never see again—the spondee for the ogre walking heavily home from his day's marauding. Picture, rhythm and feeling—when these are a unity and realized in movement, education has begun. (p. 151)

Older children can try more complicated movements such as marking the beat with the feet while clapping the rhythm with hands and then reversing the process. Eurythmy can also be practiced with rods so that if the movement is not done correctly the student's rod will clash with a neighbor's rod. These exercises, then, develop both control of the body and concentration. As the children in Grades 4 and 5 study history, myth, and legends, they can apply their learning to eurythmy. The rhythm of the Norse legends can be compared to Greek mythology. Harwood (1958) notes that the "alliterative meter of the North has a deep quality of will in it . . . while the hexameter on the other hand, is the most harmonious, the most harmonizing of all rhythms" (p. 152). By reading Homer and then doing eurythmy the students gain a much deeper feel for Greek culture than they would through a mere verbal approach.

As the child approaches adolescence, eurythmy can be related to the intellectual development of the student. For example, grammar can be explored through eurythmy as the active and passive tense can be taught through movement. Students at this age can relate more closely to music and eurythmy by having some students play their instruments while the other students do some movements.

Eurythmy is usually taught by a teacher trained in the field, but the classroom teacher is encouraged to take part in the lesson. According to Harwood: "When the eurythmy teacher is as much interested in what the children are learning in their main lessons, as the class teacher in what they are doing in movement, the children thrive in a harmony of mind and will"(p. 154). In secondary school eurythmy can be combined with drama, "perhaps in a play when there are nature spirits, as in Milton's *Comus,* or *A Midsummer Night's Dream*" (p. 155). Harwood (1958) concludes by emphasizing the importance of eurythmy in Waldorf:

> Of all elements in modern life it is the rhythmical side which is most deficient—a deficiency only too apparent in the arts today. The whole of a Waldorf education is based on rhythm, and may therefore be called curative for an age. But in this rhythmical education there is no doubt where the centre lies. It is in Eurythmy. (p. 155)

Applying Steiner's work to public education presents certain problems and opportunities. One difficulty is that his work has received little attention and there will simply have to be a great deal of work to make his ideas well known. These ideas also will have to be articulated in an open manner free from any hint of dogmatism; in other words, his theory should be viewed as a hypothesis to be tested by experience, rather than as dogma that must be followed by ritual. In an interview I did with Mary Caroline Richards, who wrote an important book on Steiner education, she said that when she reads Steiner it tends to facilitate her creativity while some of her Steiner colleagues tend to close off (Miller, 1987). For those outside the Waldorf movement we have the opportunity to look at Steiner's theory critically and also to make links with his work and other holistic approaches to education.

Steiner encouraged teachers to be creative and flexible in their approach. According to Richards (1980), they "paint and draw, sing and play recorder, recite and tell stories, and cook and play with the children" (p. 28). Steiner wanted the teacher to appeal to the interests of the child and to also use humor and surprise in the classroom. He wanted the teachers to teach from enthusiasm rather than a rigid schedule. Steiner (1976) said to teachers at the first Waldorf school before it opened:

The teacher must be a person of initiative in everything that he does, great and small. . . .

The teacher should be one who is interested in the being of the whole world and of humanity. . . .

The teacher must be one who never makes a compromise in his heart and mind with what is untrue. . . .

The teacher must never get stale or grow sour. . . .

During this fortnight I have only spoken of what can enter directly into your practical teaching, if you allow it first to work rightly within your own souls. But our Waldorf School, my dear friends, will depend upon what you do within yourselves, and whether you really allow the things which we have been considering to become effective in your own souls. . . .

I do not want to make you into teaching machines, but into free independent teachers. . . .

Let us in particular keep before us this thought which shall truly fill our hearts and minds: That bound up with the spiritual movement of the present day are also the spiritual powers that guide the Universe. If we believe in these good spiritual powers, then they will be the inspirers of our lives and we shall really be enabled to teach. (pp. 199–201)

Many elements of timeless learning are present in Waldorf education. I have already mentioned the rhythmic and flowing nature of the curriculum. The physicality of learning in Waldorf education also indicates that learning is embodied. It is also holistic in nature as the teacher works with the whole child including the spiritual side; the soul life of the child is central to Waldorf education.

Waldorf education is also connected as Steiner (1976) said that "moving from one thing to another in a way that connects one thing with another is more beneficial than anything else for the development of spirit and soul and even body" (p. 173). The main lesson which is taught every morning connects various subjects to the inner life of the child.

Mystery is also crucial to Waldorf education. Storytelling and the use of myths and legends bring mystery into the curriculum. Finally, it should be noted that assessment tends to be qualitative in nature and relies on extensive observation by the teacher rather than using paper-and-pencil tests.

MONTESSORI EDUCATION

Montessori education has spread widely since Maria Montessori began her work in Italy in the early part of the 20th century. There are several thousand Montessori schools in the United States alone.

Maria Montessori was born in 1870 and died in 1952. She lived most of her life in Italy but also spent time in Spain, India, and the Netherlands. Her original vision of education and the human being was profoundly spiritual. Montessori believed in a divine plan for the earth and the cosmos and it was humanity's duty to help in the unfolding of this plan. Within each child and person is a *spiritual embryo* that should be nurtured if the divine plan is to be realized. She wrote:

> We must believe that all human beings develop by themselves, of themselves, and that we cannot do better than not to interrupt that development. We must confess to ourselves that the psychic life of man is full of mysteries. . . . the preparation for the teacher is two fold: to be sensitive to the mystery and to be sensitive to the wonder of life revealing itself. (Cited in Buckenmeyer, 1997, p. 35)

Montessori, like Krishnamurti and Steiner, believed that within each person was the mysterious, timeless dimension. Like both men she was interested in theosophy; however, her vision of education was different.

Montessori believed in a prepared educational environment with the appropriate materials to stimulate the individual child. Her son, Mario (1992, pp. 39–41), has summarized a few of the basic principles of Montessori education:

- The aim of education is the development of the "total personality, not of independent functions or processes." In short, she held a holistic view of development.
- An optimal environment is crucial to the development of the child. Learning materials should be presented to children that allow them to work independently. The self-directed activity of the child must be respected by the teacher.

He identifies the main features of the approach:

As far as teaching is concerned, Montessori believed that the emphasis on the intellectual aspect of learning was largely wrong. The role of the personality as a psychosomatic unity in the learning process must be fully acknowledged. Not passive absorption, but intelligent action is required. Learning is a dynamic process in which the whole personality of the child must be actively engaged. The Montessori materials invite this. (p. 41)

Montessori called her approach to elementary-age children *cosmic education,* which again underlines the spiritual nature of her vision. Mario (1992) describes cosmic education when he writes: "Cosmic education seeks to offer the young, at the appropriate sensitive period, the stimulation and help they need to develop their minds, their vision, and their creative power, whatever the level or range of their personal contributions may be" (p. 101). Mario wrote that the child needs to have a "prior interest in the whole" (p. 98) so that he or she can make sense of individual facts. This can be done in part by introducing students to ecological principles that focus on the interdependence of living and nonliving things. Mario Montessori gives the example of students studying the life cycle of salmon and its relationship with the environment.

Aline Wolf (2004) has recently written about Montessori's vision of cosmic education:

Essentially Montessori's cosmic education gives the child first an all-encompassing sense of the universe with its billions of galaxies. Then it focuses on our galaxy, the Milky Way, our solar system, planet Earth and its geological history, the first specimens of life, all species of plants and animals and finally human beings. Inherent in the whole study is the interconnectedness of all creation, the oneness of things. (p. 6)

Wolf also makes reference to the work of Brian Swimme (1992) and the Universe Story which was described in Chapter 7. Cosmic education helps the child place himself or herself within the total framework of the universe. The image of the universe presented by Montessori and Swimme is one of order and purpose. Since human beings are part of the universe, it gives us a common reference point beyond the boundaries created by nations and religions.

Wolf also points out that cosmic education can help children develop a sense of reverence for life and care for the earth. Seeing the miracle of life within the vastness of the universe can help students appreciate more deeply life and the earth itself. Cosmic education can also give students a deep sense of gratitude as well:

As examples, when we see a beautiful valley nestled in the mountains, we can reflect on the fact that it was formed by water that labored thousands of years to wear down the mountainous terrain, when we enter a car or train, we can look back and feel grateful to the first human being who constructed a wheel. Awareness of the long-term cosmic pattern, of which we are only an infinitesimal part, calls us to a deep humility and reverence for all the labors of nature and the work of human beings that preceded us. (Wolf, 2004, p. 16)

Wolf suggests that cosmic education can give children a sense of meaning and purpose in their lives. As mentioned earlier, Montessori felt that within the person lies a spiritual embryo which needs to be respected and nourished so that students can eventually find their purpose on earth.

Montessori felt that silence was conducive to child development. In a speech to educators in New York in 1913 she suggested that children do not have to be active all the time but can "meditate." In her book *The Secret of Childhood* (1972) she describes an example of children meditating. She came into the classroom holding a four-month-old baby:

She was so still that her silence impressed me greatly and I wanted the children to share my feelings. "She is not making a sound" I told them. And jokingly I added, "None of you could do so well." To my great surprise I saw that the children were looking at me with an extraordinary intensity. They seemed to be hanging on my lips and to be feeling keenly what I was saying. "Notice," I continued, "how soft her breath is. None of you would breathe as silently as she." Surprised and motionless, the children began to hold their breath. At that moment there was an impressive silence. The tick-tock of the clock, which was not usually heard, began to become audible. . . . No one made the least perceptible movement. They were intent upon experiencing the silence and reproducing it. . . . The children all sat perfectly still breathing as quietly as possible, having on their faces a serene and content expression like those who are meditating. Little by little in the midst of this impressive silence we could all hear the lightest sounds like that of a drop of water falling in the distance and the far-off chirp of a bird. That was the origin of our exercise of silence. (pp. 123–124)

This exercise of silence became part of the Montessori curriculum. In her talk in New York she talked about the independent intellectual and spiritual life which lies within each child. This silent dimension of Montessori education could be seen as an example of timeless learning in her curriculum since it meant to put children in touch with the timeless essence within.

Ron Miller (2002), who was trained as a Montessori teacher, has emphasized the spiritual nature of Montessori's educational vision:

Montessori's distinctive notion of the child as a "spiritual embryo" emphasized her key principle that the growing human being is not simply a biological or psychological entity, but a spiritual energy seeking expression in the form of a human body within the cultural world. . . . Montessori, like Emerson, referred to the "secret" within the soul of every child—the personal spiritual imperative that transcends whatever social prejudices, ideologies, and mundane educational curricula that adults seek to overlay onto the child's personality. (p. 234)

Miller refers to "the genius of this brilliant woman's soaring, liberating vision" (p. 238). This vision provides another example of timeless learning and a counter to the view of education as a training ground to compete in the global economy. Montessori with her emphasis on the child's spiritual embryo and her cosmic perspective provides a framework for timeless learning.

CONCLUSION

The examples described in this chapter are in most instances private schools. There are some examples of where Waldorf and Montessori schools have been part of public school systems. For example, in Milwaukee there is a Waldorf elementary in the inner city that serves the black residents there. In the next chapter I explore how timeless learning can be brought more directly into public education. Some of the principles and ideas from Krishnamurti, Steiner, and Montessori can be adapted to public schools. Mostly, it is a matter of bringing compassion, attention, contemplation, and letting go into current pedagogical practices.

REFERENCES

Barnett, M. (1999). Learning about the self. *Natural Parent, May/June,* 36–37.

Blau, E. (1995). *Krishnamurti: 100 years.* New York: Tabori & Chang.

Buckenmeyer, R. G. (Ed.). (1997). *The California lectures of Maria Montessori, 1915: Collected speeches and writings.* Oxford, UK: ABC-Clio.

Buultjens, R. (1996). Foreword. In *Total freedom: The essential Krishnamurti.* San Francisco: Harper.

Cotton, K. (1996). *Close-up #20. School improvement research series.* Portland, OR: Northwest Regional Educational Lab.

Harwood, A. C. (1958). *The recovery of man in childhood: A study in the educational work of Rudolf Steiner.* Spring Valley, NY: Anthroposophic Press.

Kessler, S. (1991). The teaching presence. *Holistic Education Review,* 4(4), 4–15.

Kohn, A. (1993). *Punished by rewards.* Boston: Houghton Mifflin.

Krishnamurti, J. (1953). *Education and the significance of life.* New York: Harper and Row.

Krishnamurti, J. (1974). *On education.* New York: Harper & Row.

Krishnamurti, J. (1978). *Beginnings of learning.* London: Penguin Books.

Krishnamurti, J. (1996). *Total freedom: The essential Krishnamurti.* San Francisco: Harper.

Lee, V., & Smith, J. (1994). *Effects of high school restructuring on size and achievement.* Madison, WI: National Center for Organization and Restructuring of Schools.

Miller, J. (1987). *Spiritual pilgrims.* Unpublished manuscript.

Miller, J. (1996, 2001). *The holistic curriculum.* Toronto: OISE Press.

Miller, J. (2000). *Education and the soul: Toward a spiritual curriculum.* Albany, NY: State University of New York Press.

Miller, R. (2002). Nourishing the spiritual embryo: The educational vision of Maria Montessori. In J. Miller & Y. Nakagawa (Eds.), *Nurturing our wholeness: Perspectives on spirituality in education* (pp. 227–240). Brandon, VT: Foundation for Educational Renewal.

Montessori, Maria. (1972). *The secret of childhood.* New York: Ballantine.

Montessori, Mario. (1992). *Education for human development: Understanding Montessori.* Oxford, UK: Clio.

Richards, M. C. (1980). *Toward wholeness: Rudolf Steiner education in America.* Middletown, CT: Wesleyan University Press.

Sher, J. O. (1977). *Education in rural America.* Boulder, CO: Westview Press.

Steiner, R. (1975). *Education of the child in the light of anthroposophy* (G. Adams & M. Adams, Trans.). London: Rudolf Steiner Press.

Steiner, R. (1976). *Practical advice for teachers.* London: Rudolf Steiner Press.

Swimme, B., & Berry, T. (1992). *The universe story: From the primordial flaring forth to the ecozoic era—A celebration of the unfolding of the cosmos.* San Francisco: Harper.

Vernon, R. (2000). *Star in the east: Krishnamurti—the invention of a messiah.* London: Constable.

Wasley, P. (2000). *Small schools and the issue of scale.* New York: Bank Street College.

Wolf, A. (2004, October). Maria Montessori cosmic education as a nonsectarian framework for nurturing children's spirituality. Paper presented at the ChildSpirit Conference, Pacific Grove, CA.

CHAPTER NINE

Creating Conditions for Timeless Learning in Public Schools

The most important work we do is the work we do on ourselves.

—Ram Dass

Timeless learning is not limited to private schools. Every day there are teachers who are able to bring timeless learning into public school classrooms. In this chapter I explore what teachers can do to make this happen more frequently in their own schools. The suggestions should be seen as ideas to explore rather than a fixed program to be adopted.

WORK ON YOURSELF

Teachers need to work on themselves through various practices to become more present, mindful, and caring. Ram Dass and other spiritual teachers have stated the most important work that we can do is the work on ourselves. If we can be more centered and caring, then we can create a space where students may also share these qualities. Spiritual practice and timeless learning require what the Buddhists call *right effort*. In doing this work we can take a playful approach. We can truly lighten up. Again my experience with teachers I have worked with is that the work we do on ourselves begins to make a significant difference in our teaching; we are able to connect more deeply to students and their learning.

BE FULLY PRESENT

Much of the work we can do on ourselves is to be fully present. As I suggest in Chapter 6, start with the small things in your life like preparing a meal, washing the dishes, or taking a walk. Then apply this presence to the classroom. It can be a challenge in a busy classroom but your complete presence when a student speaks can be a powerful source of timeless learning. Your attention can create a psychologically safe atmosphere where students are willing to share their thoughts and feelings.

I was recently at a conference in South Africa where a black person who had formerly been involved in the resistance to apartheid gave a talk. He mentioned that a turning point in his life was when an older person listened to him. He had never experienced being listened to in this way; it made him weep. I am sure that there are many stories of how teachers listened to their students in a similar manner. Such presence and listening can be profoundly healing.

RECOGNIZE THE IMPORTANCE OF THE NONVERBAL

Diana Hughes who is head of the Teacher Education Program of the Rudolf Steiner Centre in Toronto states that holistic education occurs in that invisible space between teacher and student. It could be argued too that timeless learning also occurs in that place. What does this mean in practice? When we focus on the nonverbal, or that silent space, we become aware of how we carry ourselves, how we engage others through eye contact, and the tone of our voice. We realize that the quality of our being and presence has as much impact on student development as anything that we say. When we become aware of the nonverbal, then a balance can develop between talk and silence. At all levels, education has focused on the head and verbal exchange. We have forgotten about the rest of our bodies and how we can communicate in silence. A warm smile directed to a child can send a message of support and love.

HONOR SILENCE

Parker Palmer (1998) believes that silence is fundamental to timeless learning. If a student has said something that moves you and other students, take a few moments of silence before moving on. The Japanese have a term for the silent spaces: *ma.* Respect for *ma* involves being comfortable with the gaps and silences and not plunging ahead with more talk or activity. In the West we tend to be less comfortable with the silent spaces both in our conversation and in our teaching. Good actors know the value of silence and timing in their work and so do good teachers.

We could learn from the Quaker meeting where silence is accepted and people speak only when they are moved to do so. In our university classrooms there can be discussion without much connection to the heart. Bringing what the ancients called "the thinking heart" into our classrooms could address this problem.

DEVELOP A RHYTHM

Moving from silence to speaking can be rhythmic. As Steiner (1975) indicated, teaching and learning should have a rhythm that is not dependent on the clock; Harwood (1958) suggested that the overall rhythm in Waldorf education is one of breathing in and out.

Teachers in public schools can also develop their own teaching rhythm. This means the teacher is not stuck in one method but moves freely from one form of learning to another. Besides the rhythm of silence and speech, the teacher might move from large group learning to small group learning in a rhythmic manner. Using the framework of transmission, transaction, and transformation (see Chapter 7) also provides another way of introducing a rhythm into teaching as the teacher moves from one teaching approach to another. For example, in my classes I start with a meditation (transformation), move to a short lecture (transmission), and then have students work in small groups (transaction) around issues raised in the lecture.

INTEGRATE TIMELESS LEARNING
WITH OTHER FORMS OF LEARNING

Focusing on timeless learning does not mean throwing out other approaches (e.g., transmission and transaction) but making the effort to connect timeless learning with these other forms. For example, timeless learning can exist with strategies based on various multiple intelligences developed by Howard Gardner (1983). Timeless learning calls for an inclusive approach to teaching and learning. There has been a strong tendency in American education to adopt an either/or stance to teaching, such as progressive education vs. traditional education or whole language vs. phonics. Holistic education rejects these simplistic dichotomies and searches for ways to integrate various forms of learning.

BALANCING SPONTANEITY AND PLANNING

Developing a rhythm in our teaching involves using our intuition as teachers. Our "inner teacher" can give us clues as to when we need to change direction in the classroom.

Timeless learning does not arise in a climate that is inflexible, nor in an environment that lacks structure. Teachers should have a sense of direction that gives confidence to themselves and their students. At the same time they need to be able to shift gears when the need arises. If a student or group of students raises an issue or topic that clearly interests them, then this issue can be addressed. This is the teachable moment that was described in the previous chapter.

DON'T FORGET THE BODY

At all age levels we cannot ignore our bodies. Encourage simple exercises where students can focus on what the body is experiencing as they go through the learning process. This can be done by having students notice their breathing as Montessori did in her classroom or through various exercises such as the body scan which was described in Chapter 4.

The witness is helpful in remembering the body. The witness is that place in our consciousness that is watching in a nonjudgmental manner. It can see when our body begins to tense up. As soon as this happens, we can take a deep breath or consciously relax our muscles.

LIVE YOUR OWN TRUTH

Parker Palmer (1998) states that the ultimate approach to teaching is simply "living your own truth." He calls this approach the heart's reward. Look then to living your own truth rather than seeking external approval or recognition for your teaching. Teaching is much more than seeing students do well on a test although achievement certainly has its place. Instead, teaching is fraught with ambiguity and uncertainty as to what impact we are having. Sometimes we only find out years later when we run into students and they tell about the impact we had on their life. But if we are living what Palmer calls the "undivided life," we find a deep and rich reward inside us. There is a deep sense of fulfillment which is the ultimate reward.

ACKNOWLEDGE THE MYSTERY

Within each student is a mysterious destiny. Carl Jung said: "I simply believe that some part of the human Self or Soul is not subject to the laws of space and time" (cited in Winokur, 1990, p. 73). Our simple awareness of this aspect of humanity can lead to true empowerment. We empower our students when we can acknowledge this aspect in their lives; if we do not then it may not be released. In the gnostic Gospels Jesus is quoted as saying: "If you bring forth what is within you, what you bring forth will save you. If you do not bring forth what is within you, what you do not bring forth will destroy you" (cited in Pagels, 1979, p. xv). If we are not sensitive to what is within the student it may not be brought forth. Timeless learning then attempts to connect with and nurture this part of the human being which is so often neglected in our classrooms.

I recently had a student in my class who I had found slightly annoying. She missed some classes and wanted an extension on her paper; I felt she was not really engaged in the course. It was not till I read her paper that I realized how much the course had meant to her. She had been suffering from an eating disorder and in her paper she described how the course had been helpful in her healing process. She reminded me how the Mystery that resides within each student can both surprise me and teach me to suspend my judgment.

LET YOUR HUMANITY COME THROUGH

In my classes I ask the teachers to give me an example of holistic education. Often they cite cases where they went on camping trips with the students or other activities where the role of teacher changed from instructor to guide. In this role the student could see the teacher more as a human being and the bond between the teacher and the students was strengthened.

Teachers should not be afraid to talk about their own lives. Share incidents that happen in your life that you think might be of interest to the students. Rachael Kessler telling her class about not being able to get home because of the fire is a good example of this.

Finally, do not be afraid to show emotion. Years ago beginning teachers were told "do not smile till Christmas"; instead I think teachers should laugh. Even better if they can laugh at themselves. Chesterton once wrote: "Angels can fly because they take themselves lightly" (cited in Winokur, 1990, p. 38). Teachers who can take themselves lightly can touch the angelic nature of their students.

REFERENCES

Emerson, R. W. (1990). *Selected, essays, lectures and poems.* New York: Bantam.

Gardner, H. (1983). *Frames of mind.* New York: Basic Books.

Harwood, A. C. (1958). *The recovery of man in childhood: A study in the educational work of Rudolf Steiner.* Spring Valley, NY: Anthroposophic Press.

Pagels, E. (1979). *The gnostic Gospels.* New York: Vintage Books.

Palmer, P. (1998). *The courage to teach: Exploring the inner landscape of a teacher's life.* San Francisco: Jossey-Bass.

Steiner, R. (1975). *Education of the child in the light of anthroposophy* (G. Adams & M. Adams, Trans.). London: Rudolf Steiner Press.

Winokur, J. (1990). *Zen to go.* New York: Penguin Books.

CHAPTER TEN

The Fruits of Timeless Learning

The most evident token and apparent sign of true wisdom is a constant and unconstrained rejoicing.

—Montaigne

THE PRESENT EDUCATIONAL CONTEXT

How can timeless learning address the most pressing issues in education today? Tobin Hart (2004) has recently identified three major issues that dominate today's educational discourse: student performance, the development of character, and the need for depth in the curriculum. He claims that contemplative approaches can address these issues; it can also be argued that timeless learning which is rooted in contemplative approaches also addresses these issues.

Perhaps the most ubiquitous issue is student performance and accountability. The call for testing at every grade level and the demand for high stakes testing seem unending. Hart cites the research of Winter (2002) that suggests that high stakes testing may actually worsen student performance.

There is a great deal of research that suggests that contemplative practices improve performance in many areas (Murphy & Donovan, 1997; Murphy, 1992). Educators have basically ignored this research and this is probably due to the fact that North American culture is not particularly comfortable with silence and contemplative practices.

However, there have been signs of change in the last couple of years. Both *Time* (2003) and *Newsweek* (2004) have featured cover stories on meditation and the mind-body connection. Both issues cited extensive research on the positive benefits of meditation and mindfulness practices.

Timeless learning is also relevant to the issue of character. Although this is a difficult area to research, wisdom traditions have long maintained that timeless learning can lead to joy, wholeness, awe and wonder, and a sense of purpose. Certainly our society could benefit from students who have developed some of these qualities. So much of schooling is focused narrowly on achievement in school subjects rather than on nurturing the whole human being. We desperately need to expand our vision of education, and timeless learning offers the opportunity to expand the vision.

Regarding the issue of depth, I have already briefly discussed slow education as one example of timeless learning that addresses this issue. Both slow education and holistic education reject the fast-food approach to learning.

THE RESULTS OF TIMELESS LEARNING

In this chapter I address issues that Hart and others have raised by looking at the fruits, or outcomes, of timeless learning. The short term outcomes coming out of contemplative practices are supported by a large body of research while the long term outcomes such as joy and wholeness have been articulated by sacred literature, the arts, and poetry.

First, we examine some of the research on attention-based practices such as meditation since this has been identified as one of the central aspects of timeless learning. A substantial amount of evidence has been collected to indicate the positive outcomes of meditation.

RESEARCH ON CONTEMPLATIVE PRACTICES

The physiological and psychological benefits to meditation are well documented. Murphy (1992; Murphy & Donovan, 1997) has summarized these benefits from over 1,300 studies. Some of the benefits include lowered heart rate, reduce blood pressure, heightened perception, increased empathy, anxiety reduction, relief from addiction, alleviation of pain, and improvements in memory and learning ability. Meditation has also been linked to the reversal of heart disease. Along with other changes such as improvements in diet and exercise, Dean Ornish (1990) has found that meditation is an important factor in reversing heart illness.

Roger Walsh (1999) has summarized some of the research on several of aspects of timeless learning including developing attention and compassion. He puts these practices under the label of Asian therapies and concludes that "experimental evidence clearly demonstrates that Asian therapies can ameliorate a broad range of psychological and psychosomatic difficulties . . . and enhance psychological growth and well being" (p. 104).

The research on using contemplative practices in schools is much more limited. However Gina Levete (1995) cites some studies that indicate the positive benefits of meditation for students. In one study, at a boys' school in the Middle East, secondary school students were split into two groups. The experimental groups meditated for the entire year on a daily basis and it was found that they performed better academically than the control group which did not meditate (p. 2). A study released by the University of Michigan also found some interesting results for African American sixth grade students. In a controlled study, students who did transcendental meditation reported increased positive affectivity, self-esteem, and emotional competence (Benn, 2003).

MY OWN RESEARCH

My own experience introducing meditation to teachers is congruent with the findings of Murphy and Walsh. Along with a colleague, Ayako Nozawa, we carried out a qualitative study on teachers who have taken my courses in holistic education. Students are introduced to six different types of meditation, which include meditation on the breath, loving-kindness (sending thoughts of peace and wellness to self and others), mantra, movement (e.g., walking), visualization, and contemplation on poetry or sacred texts. Some students work out their own forms and integrate meditation with their own spiritual and religious practice. Although sitting meditation is encouraged, some students do movement meditation. For example, one student swam every day, as he approached swimming with a mindful awareness. Whatever form students choose, meditation can be seen as letting go of the *calculating mind* and opening to the *listening mind* which tends to be characterized by a *relaxed alertness*. Once the students have settled on a method they are encouraged to work up to about 30 minutes a day of meditation practice. I keep in touch with each student through a journal they keep on their practice.

Each class begins with the loving-kindness meditation (see Chapter 5) and students are encouraged to begin or end their own individual meditation with it. Finally, students are also introduced to *mindfulness* practice which was described in Chapter 6.

To date over 1,300 students have been introduced to meditation practice in these courses. Only two students in 16 years have asked not to do the assignment. So far there has not been one student who has reported an overall negative experience with the practice during the course. Most of the students are women (80%) in their late 20s, 30s, or 40s. While most of the students come from Ontario, there have also been students from Brazil, China, Indonesia, Iran, Italy, Jamaica, Lebanon, Japan, Kenya, Korea, and Malta.

Students are asked to meditate each day for six weeks. In the beginning, they meditate for about 10 to 15 minutes a day, and by the end of the six weeks they are encouraged to meditate 20 to 30 minutes. Students are required to keep a journal which focuses on how the process of meditation is going (e.g., how the concentration and focus are going, how the body is feeling, etc.). The journals also focus on how meditation has affected them. Some of themes have included:

- Giving themselves permission to be alone and enjoy their own company;
- Increased listening capacities;
- Feeling increased energy;
- Being less reactive to situations and generally experiencing greater calm and clarity.

At the end of the process they write a reflective summary of the experience. Below is an excerpt from one of these summaries. One woman who has dealt with illness writes:

When I meditate I concentrate on the internal organs and the sensations they feel. I practice lovingkindness to my internal organs and actually speak to them. This seems strange but effective. I ask them to forgive me for not listening earlier to their signals of exhaustion or distress. . . .

Meditation offers a tremendous sense of release. It is my own sanctuary and anchor during times of stress. I relish the fact that I can detach during times of stress and anxiety and practice being in the moment. I can focus on my present surroundings and be mindful. . . .

I am aware of my yin/yang or feminine/masculine side. My masculine side is flourishing because I'm allowing it the space to speak to me during meditation. This has given me more confidence.

My heart hungers for beauty in nature and I have become more aware and mindful. My senses are acute and feed my soul when I am in the park. It is almost as if I reach another state of being—the smell of the earth and dried leaves, the coolness of the breeze, the touch of bark and leaves, the gentle warmth of the sun, the ducks and blue herons in the pond. . . .

Most important is the sacredness of human life. I tell my husband and children that they are so sacred. Sometimes I look at total stranger's walk, clothing or mannerisms. Something about that person moves me intuitively. . . . I am overcome with a sense of compassion and love that is unexplainable. Meditation allows me to be me without any conditions.

This study described here was conducted as a follow-up to people who had done the meditation in one of the courses mentioned above. The study focused on the following questions:

1. What is the nature of your meditation practice? (e.g., type and frequency)

2. Have you engaged in any meditation instruction since the class?

3. What have been the effects of your practice on your personal and professional life?

4. Have you experienced any difficulties or problems with the practice?

Letters were sent out to 182 former students asking if they would be interested in participating in an interview related to the questions above. Because the study involved a face-to-face interview, it was limited to former students living in the Toronto area. From this group 40 letters were returned. In the end 21 former students (17 women and 4 men) agreed to participate. Of the 21, 11 were teachers at the elementary or secondary level, 4 were teaching at the postsecondary level, 4 were administrators, and 2 were consultants.

Nature of Meditation Practice

For the large majority of individuals (19 of 21) introduction to meditation came in the course; however, two individuals had already been meditating when they enrolled in the course. One person had taken the course seven years ago, while seven had taken the course as recently as two years ago. The average length of time meditating for the participants was a little over four years.

Effects of Meditation Practice

All the participants except one commented on the positive effects of the practice on their personal and professional lives.

Personal Effects of Meditation Practice

The majority of participants (13, or 62%) commented on how the meditation had helped them become calmer and more relaxed. Some of the comments included:

> I've noticed I'm calmer. I'm much calmer. (female vice principal)
>   There is a sense of feeling more centered, more whole, calmer, more peaceful, more contented, or grounded. (male teacher)
>   I'm not as agitated . . . or I'm not as arousable from the point of view that things don't bother me as much. . . . I feel calmer, I feel more . . . this word centered keeps coming to mind. (female nursing professor)

A few participants talked about how the process of being mindful brought calmness into their daily life:

> The mindfulness is also a very powerful concept for me. It's really helping. It changed my life a lot. . . . I know that I'm less anxious and I'm less worried. (female teacher)

I will go into the park and I will park the car and I will just stare out at the trees. And I will just open the window so I hear the natural sounds. I don't have the radio on. And just become conscious of my breathing. (male consultant)

I find these little moments kind of funny when they happen because all of a sudden I become very aware that I'm washing the dishes or vacuuming. . . . And I kind of get into the moment, and it stays with me during the day. (female administrator)

Another main effect noted by five participants was that they felt that the meditation softened them or made them more gentle. One female teacher who does walking meditation commented:

It makes me gentle. And I also find that I'm feeling angry or upset about something, and then I walk, then by the end of the walk—it doesn't carry the same power over me anymore.

Another woman stated:

It made a difference in softening me in my home, in my personal life in terms of working through the process with my husband and, you know, how do you solve this? (female principal)

Finally, five participants felt that the meditation had helped them with personal relationships. One female administrator commented:

It affects all your relationships. They're better. They're deeper.

A male consultant found that people come to him for help:

Well a lot of my friends, they phone me for advice. I'm sort of like their counselor, because once you get into that whole realm of awareness and meditation and looking at things in perspective. . . .

Professional Effects of Meditation Practice

Again more than half the participants commented on how the meditation helped them be calmer in the workplace. One principal commented how calmness is important to the whole process of change, "And to get any kind of change happening in schools, it's imperative that people are calm and are in an almost meditative state in order to make those changes that are being demanded." This principal runs meetings that don't have an agenda so that "We're just here to talk about the work that we're doing, and enjoy each other." She adds this is "not team building, it's just kind of being together, it doesn't have a name."

The participants commented that a related effect is that they are not as reactive as they step back from troublesome situations:

> You can get really frustrated with these kids because these kids get really angry and frustrated because they can't read, and your first response is to be an authoritarian, when in actuality they just need to be hugged and loved. So it (the meditation) really helps me to step back and look at what really is going on. (female teacher)

Another teacher simply said:

> I don't remember the last time I raised my voice.

She added that one of her students told her:

> Miss, how come you're so calm all the time?

One of the most interesting effects was the way four of the teachers integrated the meditation into their teaching. One teacher who teaches Grades 5 and 6 along with Grade 8 drama says:

> I've been doing it now since Jack's course, so I've been doing it for three years, with all the kids, especially in drama, the meditation's amazing, and they love it, they ask me now . . . They'll come in . . . and now my students ask me, "Can we meditate, we're really hyper." Or "Can we meditate before the test?"

This teacher has the students focus on the breathing as a way to focus and relax. She also has them visualize going to the beach or lying on a cloud. She integrates the visualization with her teaching so that if they are reading a novel in class she will have them imagine some aspect of the story. In studying ancient civilizations she had them close their eyes and see the pyramids and feel sand blowing on their faces. She sees the impact in their art and poetry. "I mean I've never seen such poetry. Just with more colorful vocabulary. Colorful words, colorful language."

Another teacher at the high school has introduced meditation to approximately 1,500 students. She teaches in the Catholic system and in seven years she has never received a complaint from a parent. She explains how she introduces meditation:

> I first create a very safe environment in my class, so people feel very comfortable. . . . And then we get to a point where I'm saying, "Now there's a different way to pray. Usually, in our tradition, we mean we need to talk to God, or to the Higher Spirit, but sometimes we need to sit and listen. . . . So this is a form to connect with your spirit" . . . And I have my students' journal as well. So I ask for journal reflections and they're very powerful. And now word gets around, because people come to my class the first day and say, "Are we going to meditate today?"

A teacher who works with students training to be teachers has attempted to integrate the mindfulness and loving-kindness into his teaching. He says "I'm encouraging my classes to take joy in the tasks that are not necessarily glamorous . . . and the whole loving-kindness notion is that any kind of direction you give is simply a suggestion in loving way."

Another individual who taught Grades 4 to 8 in the Catholic system also introduced meditation to her students. Like the secondary school teacher, she connected the meditation to prayer. She found that if she missed a day of meditation, the students would insist on doing it. She said that the supply teacher who took over her class told the principal that her classes were always very calm:

> And I'm not a very calm type of teacher. I'm a very active kind of teacher, and I have everybody doing different things. . . . But I'm sure it's meditation, I can't prove it, but I'm sure it's that thing that brings us together. And it connects—you connect on a different level, you know not just the intellectual. But you connect on a spiritual level and when we were like that in our classroom the supply teacher would notice: This is a very calm classroom.

Profiles

Claire

Claire first took the course in 1993. Claire is a special education teacher at the intermediate level. Below are some excerpts from her journal from that course. She starts by focusing on the breath and counting the breath. As they are for most beginners, the first weeks were sometimes frustrating for Claire:

> Distracted! I don't get this . . . my environment is certainly cooperating, a silent house, my dog curled at my feet. I try to maintain focus, finding the counting to be a comforting anchor but after a few breaths I find myself fidgeting.

For the rest of the course she practiced visualization and some walking meditation which is the meditation that she does today. In a later entry she notes:

> It feels like whatever I do I am doing it bigger, or more, or deeper or something—especially walking . . . it is strong and rhythmic with my movement and my breathing synchronizing.

Now Claire walks almost every day for 45 minutes. She usually takes her dog for the walk. When she begins the walk, she often prays for 10 minutes or so about issues that are confronting her that day. The prayer usually also includes thanking God for the blessings in her life. After that she settles into a rhythm for the rest of the walk:

> I get a pace with my walking that matches my breath so that it's just a comfortable, familiar place that I know. I know when I've hit it. It's just the way the breath goes in and comes out is at peace with the way that I walk. And when I get to that place, I feel that's the part where I feel myself becoming still.

She describes this place further:

> I just feel the process brings me to a place of gratitude, brings me to a place of peacefulness, and calm and stillness. And also to a place where I feel I'm enough, that I'm just fine, that I'm enough.

The walking meditation has become part of Claire's life. She says:

> It carries its own momentum. When you practice it becomes easier to practice. Because once you're doing it, and you set that time aside and you honor it, you get used to having it. The longing for it.

Claire feels that the walking meditation helps her feel grounded in her work. She says: "I interact with others more calmly, more gently, more compassionately." Claire works with kids who have behavioral difficulties and who are often angry. She notes:

I feel a patience with them and tenderness towards them. . . . The kid is being rude—driving me crazy. Instead, I see the kid is hurting and I care for him differently. I think I see the student as myself.

Claire also works on being mindful in the classroom and being present to her students. The meditation and mindfulness helps bring Claire to a deep sense of connectedness:

And that place of gentleness, and presence, and mindfulness, breathing and really living in some healthy way of connecting, well, it connects you with yourself, but it also connects you to those around you. I mean there's a sense of common soul. There's just a sense that we are all just one.

Mary

Mary is counselor and special needs consultant working in a community college. She works with students who have learning disabilities.

Mary took the course in 1995. Her meditation practice is insight, or *vipassana,* described in Chapter 4. After starting the practice, Mary faced a battle with cancer. She then supplemented her vipassana meditation with visualization where she would imagine the healthy cells battling the cancerous cells. Eventually though she just returned to the vipassana meditation.

Mary meditates for about 30 minutes three or four times a week but also when she is feeling stress. For example, she meditated on the operating table before her surgery for cancer. She has also meditated in special places such as the Grand Canyon and Pacific Ocean. Mary has supplemented her practice by attending a meditation retreat and also a program that included meditation offered at the hospital where she has been treated for the cancer. Mary also practices *Qi Gong,* which is a form of movement meditation.

Mary feels meditation has had a deep impact on her life. She says: "It's totally affected my personal life. It's enabled me to live in the present. . . . I find when I go for a walk now, I am so busy looking at everything that's around me and I'm not thinking." Mary sees the impermanence of things including her own thoughts. She finds it helpful to name thoughts as they arise so that if she has an angry thought she will label that thought "angry." This process helps her let go of negative thoughts.

In her work she finds that she is much more present to students when they come to her. She also finds that she is more compassionate and believes that both the meditation and her illness have led to the compassion. She feels that her ego does not get in the way in the workplace. For example, someone who is actually below her in the college hierarchy was telling her how to do her job. While other coworkers resented this, she said it didn't bother her at all. She also finds now that she simply wants the best for everyone she meets and works with.

> I never think someone has more than I have or someone is better off, even people who are well. I don't begrudge them their health anymore, I'm happy for them. And so the meditation may have helped here, because you become one with the larger whole that happens. . . . Meditation has made me better able to show love to other people. You know I was quite reserved before. Again the illness and meditation have probably contributed here.

Mary also recites a poem that she finds helpful in her daily life.

> I have arrived, I am home,
> In the here, in the now
> I am solid, I am free

Although one cannot generalize from a qualitative study, this study does indicate that power of teachers working on themselves through contemplative practices.

ULTIMATE OUTCOMES OF TIMELESS LEARNING

Some of the participants in the study refer to the long term effects of meditation practice which are difficult to assess from a quantitative perspective. Still I believe that these are the most important fruits of timeless learning.

Goals and outcomes cannot be guaranteed from practicing timeless learning; rather they are seen as possibilities or probabilities. Without getting into lengthy and difficult discussion of causality we need to recognize that indeterminacy and nonlocality tend to be an inherent part of relationship. Gordon (2003) summarizes this concept:

> We begin to see that unpredictability and uncertainty do indeed follow universal laws once we accept that probability is not an expression of ignorance but rather accurately reflects the web-like patterns of interconnection that we see all around us in the natural world. (p. 104)

Still we can look to the wisdom traditions for the possible fruits of spiritual practice and timeless learning. These include: *wisdom and compassion; a deep and profound joy (the singing soul); awe and wonder for life and the earth; wholeness of mind, body, and spirit; and a sense of purpose in one's life.*

Wisdom and Compassion

The ancients referred to wisdom as the "thinking heart." The thinking heart means that intelligence is not just limited to the brain. Recent research on the heart supports the ancient insight (McCraty & Childre, 2002). This research has been conducted in large part by the Institute of HeartMath and suggests that:

> It is now well established that the heart is far more than a simple pump. It also functions as a hormonal gland, a sensory organ, and an information-encoding and -processing center, with an extensive intrinsic nervous system sufficiently sophisticated to qualify as a "heart brain." (Arguelles, McCraty, & Rees, 2003, p. 14)

Some of this research has found that a "smooth, sine-wave-like pattern in heart rhythms" contributes to an overall state of physiological coherence that is associated with the experience of positive emotions. The Institute of HeartMath also identifies a number of practices to facilitate this coherence that can be seen as variations on contemplative practices. The HeartMath activities have been used in a variety of school settings and it was found that these led to improved anger management skills and improved relationships with teachers, family, and peers. Other studies have shown increases in academic achievement (McCraty, Tomasino, Atkinson, Aasen, & Thurik, 2000).

It should be noted, however, that the goal of timeless learning and associated practices is not just improving test scores but realizing these deeper and longer lasting outcomes. Attaining wisdom is a lifetime project which should begin in an education system that acknowledges the ancient goal of human wholeness.

Joy: The Singing Soul

Timeless learning leads to a deep sense of joy. Robert Sardello (1992) refers to this joy as *the singing soul*:

> Soul learning does not consist of the internalization of knowledge, the determination of right meaning, the achievement of accuracy, but is to be found in what sounds right. That the soul sings was understood by the ancient psychology of the soul of the world— the singing of soul was known as the music of the spheres. (p. 63)

We can see the singing soul in people like Nelson Mandela and the Dalai Lama. The Dalai Lama's laughter and Mandela's warm smile are expressions of the singing soul. Perhaps there is no better example of the singing soul than William Blake who sang on his deathbed. He sang "Hallelujahs & songs of joy & Triumph. . . . He sang loudly & with true extatic energy and seemed, too, happy that he had finished his course, that he had ran his race & that he was shortly to arrive at the Goal" (cited in King, 1991, p. 228).

Montaigne once wrote that "The most evident token and apparent sign of true wisdom is a constant and unconstrained rejoicing" (cited in *The Secrets of Joy,* 1995, p. 125). This joy comes from deep within. Emerson (2003) wrote: "I will so trust that what is deep is holy, that I will do strongly before the sun and moon whatever only rejoices me and the heart appoints" (p. 283).

One teacher who had been doing mindfulness practice said that students thought she seemed happier. Classrooms and schools that practice various forms of timeless learning will be places where students are happy and enjoy being there.

In her book, *Schools Where Children Matter,* Doralice De Souza Rocha (2003) describes a school where children experience real joy. One parent describes how her child feels:

> He wakes up early in the morning and he is like "is it time for school?" He gets really upset with us if we are running a little slow. . . . And he just hardly waits to get to school everyday. . . . The school breaks are very long for him, because he is waiting to go back to school. In public school it was totally opposite. He would cry and say "I can't go to school, I don't want to go!" (p. 156)

Schools where timeless learning occurs are places where students want to be. Emerson (2003) wrote that "Nothing great is ever achieved without enthusiasm" (p. 324); so too with learning and our children. Too often classrooms at all levels of the education system become places where students are inoculated into passivity and boredom.

Awe and Wonder

Michael Lerner (2000) has stated that awe and wonder should be the first goals of education. Emerson believed that all human beings have an inherent right to an original relationship to the universe. It is out of this original relationship that awe and wonder naturally manifest. Witnessing nature can give rise to this relationship; for example, watching the clouds move in the sky, seeing a starry night, and observing birds in flight. Many of us living in cities have lost this relationship, or it has become mediated through television or a computer screen. Timeless learning then attempts to provide unmediated experiences in the natural world. Some of activities described in Chapter 5 with regard to caring nurture this sense of awe and reverence. Awe and wonder, however, can also arise through other activities; the arts can be another source through music, visual arts, poetry, and dance (Miller, 2000).

Timeless learning seeks then to restore a natural sense of wonder in children and ourselves as parents and teachers. It is not something that can be manipulated; instead, we can provide the settings and conditions where awe and wonder can arise.

Waldorf teachers attempt to cultivate this sense in children as students recite verses and sing songs that focus on appreciating things we often take for granted such as the air, sun, and water. The

Waldorf teacher often will talk about the materials that the students are working with. For example, if the student is working with wool the teacher will explain where it came from so that the children do not just see the wool as an object but as gift from the sheep. One biology teacher in a public high school could always identify the students from a Waldorf school because they would ask about where the frogs that they were dissecting came from.

Wholeness

Wholeness refers to recognizing the interconnected nature of experience and the multidimensionality of human beings. Timeless learning fosters this awareness in ourselves and our students. We see the relationship between the physical, intellectual, emotional, and spiritual dimensions within ourselves and others.

Wholeness also includes accepting the shadow within. It does not mean creating some ideal model of the human being and trying to live up to that model. Instead, it calls for acceptance for all that happens to us in the moment, which can include suffering, ignorance, and misunderstanding. The tendency in our culture has been to repress our shadow side. Acceptance does not mean glorification of our neuroses, just an awareness that they are there. This awareness can be the beginning of healing.

Our education system has focused on the intellect and ignored the body, emotions, and spirit. We pay the price every day in our culture with physical and emotional sickness. Obesity has become a major problem in our culture and our schools give little attention to nutrition and exercise. The ethical problems that we see in our corporations can be seen as a natural outgrowth of an educational system that focuses primarily on testing, competition, and individual achievement.

The vision of human wholeness is an ancient one. It can be found in the worldview of indigenous peoples, in Greek culture, in Buddhism, Hinduism, and Taoism, and in the American transcendentalists. Each element in our body is interconnected and our bodies are connected to all that surrounds us. These interconnections form the whole. Marcus Aurelius (1997) saw this:

> This you must always bear in mind, what is the nature of the whole, and what is my nature, and how this is related to that, and

what kind of part it is of what kind of a whole; and that there is no one who hinders you from always doing and saying the things that conform to the nature of which you are part. (p. 9)

I believe that we desperately need to reclaim this ancient vision and reframe it in terms of our own time and culture.

Sense of Purpose

Timeless learning can lead to a sense that our lives are not random events but have meaning both personally and within a larger cosmic context. In a Taoistic sense, when we engage in spiritual practice and timeless learning we can find that we align ourselves with the *way* of things. This *way*, or the Tao, underlies all that is, and when we feel a part of this way a deep sense of fulfillment and purpose can arise. *Purpose* is used here in the broadest sense. It does not refer to immediate purposes and goals but rather to the alignment of our lives with this larger way. This sense is expressed by Laurence Boldt (1999):

Moving from the *unity* of the *Tao,* from the experience of oneness with all of life, we receive the *natural* abundance of the universe with ease in a spirit of gratitude and joy. Thus the energy *flows* freely in our lives, and we fulfill our innate destinies. Recognizing the innate *power* and dignity of all of life, we live in *harmony* with it and its natural cycles. Respecting our humanity above any outer goal or reward, we cultivate the sense of leisure and peace necessary to appreciate the *beauty* and order inherent in life, and thus, allow it to express itself through us in all we do. (p. 12)

Boldt (1999) discusses the creative life which is in harmony with the natural order of things. Sometimes our lives can seem very difficult and even chaotic but when we look back we can begin to decipher an order. Schopenhauer, when he was in his sixties, looked back on his life and recognized an order, "a pattern so intricate that it suggested the narrative of a well-written story" (p. 261). This organic pattern in Taoism is called the *li.* Boldt suggests this natural pattern is "there all the while, whether we choose to ignore or embrace it" (p. 261).

Timeless learning encourages us to embrace the *li.* Lives lived in ignorance of *li* along with the forces of greed and materialism present an immense challenge for us today. Boldt (1999) cites a story about an old man living on the south coast of China who said at the end of the 20th century: "Before, people acted according to ethics of Confucianism, then according to the precepts of Communism; today, people are just greedy" (p. 59). The last phrase applies equally well to life in North America. We seem to live our lives in a way described by Will Rogers: "Too many people spend money they haven't earned, to buy things they don't want, to impress people they don't like" (cited in Boldt, 1999, p. 44).

Education that recognizes the importance of timeless learning would provide an alternative approach that could help us restore sanity to our lives and our culture. It would help us to begin to bring a deeper meaning, joy, and purpose to our lives. Can we really afford not to explore such an alternative?

Finally, in these days of accountability, outcomes, and expectations, it is interesting to look at the outcomes for doing loving-kindness which were identified over 2,000 years ago by the Buddha (cited in Salzberg, 1995). Some of these benefits include:

- You will sleep easily.
- You will wake easily.
- You will have pleasant dreams.
- People and animals will love you.
- Your face will be radiant.
- Your mind will be serene.
- You will die unconfused.

I have witnessed several of these benefits in my students who have practiced loving-kindness and mindfulness. These are truly outcomes that could lead to the healing of ourselves and the planet. They provide perhaps the most powerful argument for timeless learning.

REFERENCES

Arguelles, L., McCraty, R., & Rees, R. (2003). The heart of holistic education. *Encounter: Education for Meaning And Social Justice, 16*(3), 13–21.

Aurelius, M. (1997). *Meditations* (W. Kaufmann, Ed.). Mineola, NY: Dover.

Benn, R. (2003). *Preliminary results of pilot study: Effects of transcendental meditation on social emotional development in early adolescence.* Abstract retrieved March 21, 2005, from http://www.med.umich.edu/opm/newspage/2003/meditationstatement.htm

Boldt, L. G. (1999). *The Tao of abundance: Eight principles for abundant living*. New York: Penguin.

De Souza Rocha, D. L. (2003). *Schools where children matter: Exploring educational alternatives*. Brandon VT: Foundation for Educational Renewal.

Emerson, R. W. (2003). *Selected writings* (W. H. Gilman, Ed.). New York: Signet.

Gordon, K. (2003). The impermanence of being: Towards a psychology of uncertainty. *Journal of Humanistic Psychology, 43*(2), 96–117.

Hart, T. (2004). Opening the contemplative mind in the classroom. *Journal of Transformative Education, 2*(1), 28–46.

Kalb, C. (2004). Buddha lessons: A technique called mindfulness teaches how to step back from pain and the worries of life. *Newsweek, CXLIV*(13), 48–51.

King, J. (1991). *William Blake: A life*. London: Weidenfeld and Nicolson.

Lerner, M. (2000). *Spirit matters*. Charlottesville, VA: Hampton Roads.

Levete, G. (1995). *Presenting the case for meditation in primary and secondary schools*. Unpublished manuscript.

McCraty, R., & Childre, D. (2002). *The appreciative heart: The psychophysiology of positive emotions and optimal functioning*. Boulder Creek, CA: HeartMath Research Center.

McCraty, R., Tomasino, D., Atkinson, M., Aasen, P., & Thurik, S. J. (2000). *Improving test taking skills and academic performance in high school students using HeartMath learning enhancement tools*. Boulder Creek, CA: HeartMath Research Center.

Miller, J. (2000). *Education and the soul: Toward a spiritual curriculum*. Albany: SUNY Press.

Murphy, M. (1992). *The future of the body: Explorations into the further evolution of human nature*. New York: Jeremy P. Tarcher.

Murphy, M., & Donovan, S. (1997). *The physical and psychological effects of meditation*. Sausalito, CA: Institute of Noetic Sciences.

Ornish, D. (1990). *Dr. Dean Ornish's program for recovering from heart disease*. New York: Random House.

Salzberg, S. (1995). *Lovingkindness: The revolutionary art of happiness*. Boston: Shambhala.

Sardello, R. (1992). *Facing the world with soul*. Hudson, NY: Lindisfarne Press.

The secrets of joy: A treasury of wisdom. (1995). Philadelphia: Running Press.

Stein, J. (2003). Just say om. *Time, 162*(5), 38–46.

Walsh, R. (1999). Asian contemplative disciplines: Common practices, clinical applications and research findings. *Journal of Transpersonal Psychology, 31*(2), 83–108.

Winter, G. (2002, December 28). More schools rely on tests, but study raises doubts. *New York Times*, p. A1.

Bibliography

Bickman, M. (2003). *Minding American education: Reclaiming the tradition of active learning.* New York: Teachers College Press.

This is an excellent historical overview of holistic education with interesting chapters on Emerson, Thoreau, Alcott, and Dewey.

De Souza Rocha, D. (2003). *Schools where children matter: Exploring educational alternatives.* Brandon VT: Foundation for Educational Renewal.

Doralice De Souza Rocha, an educational researcher from Brazil, examines three different schools with a holistic approach to education. Included in her analysis is an insightful look at Waldorf education.

Glazer, S. (1999). *The heart of learning: Spirituality in education.* New York: Tarcher/Putnam.

This book is a collection of papers presented at a major conference held on spirituality in education at Naropa University. Contributors include the Dalai Lama, bell hooks, Huston Smith, and Parker Palmer.

Hanh, T. N. (1976). *The miracle of mindfulness: A manual on meditation.* Boston: Beacon.

This is a classic in the field of mindfulness meditation and is filled with a variety of mindfulness activities.

Hart, T. (2001). *From information to transformation: Education for the evolution of consciousness.* New York: Peter Lang.

Tobin Hart has become one of the leading voices in the spirituality-in-education movement. In this book he approaches concepts such as wisdom and transformation and how they can be manifested in our education.

Hart, T. (2003). *The secret spiritual world of children.* Makawo, HI: Inner Ocean.

This book is the result of five years of interviewing children and adults about the spiritual lives of children. It contains fascinating stories of children's inner wisdom as well as of how teachers and parents can nurture this wisdom.

Horton, M. (1998). *The long haul: An autobiography.* New York: Teachers College Press.

Myles Horton was cofounder of the Highlander Center. He was both a holistic educator and social activist. His book is a must-read on how holistic education and social activism can be integrated.

Kessler, R. (2000). *The soul of education: Helping students find connection, compassion, and character in school.* Alexandria, VA: Association for Supervision and Curriculum Development.

This book is based on Rachael Kessler's years of experience working with adolescents and on how their longing for spiritual connection can be addressed in public schools.

Kohn, A. (1999). *The schools our children deserve: Moving beyond traditional classrooms and "tougher standards."* Boston: Houghton Mifflin.

Alfie Kohn challenges today's conventional educational policies by arguing for a more holistic approach to education. Kohn supports his case with extensive references to current research.

Krishnamurti, J. (1953). *Education and the significance of life.* New York: Harper & Row.

This book is Krishnamurti's most powerful statement on education; it outlines his vision in clear and accessible language. It is a classic in the field of holistic learning.

Levete, G. (1995). *Presenting the case for meditation in primary and secondary schools.* Unpublished paper.

Gina Levete has been working to bring meditation into schools in England and this short booklet summarizes her efforts and research.

Marshak, D. (1997). *The common vision: Parenting and educating for wholeness.* New York: Peter Lang.

This is another must-read in the holistic education literature. Marshak examines the work of Sri Aurobindo Ghose, Rudolf Steiner, and Hazrat Inayat Kahn. He identifies their common vision of human development and its implications for education.

Miller, J. (1994). *The contemplative practitioner: Meditation in education and the professions.* Westport, CT: Bergin and Garvey.

This book focuses on the contemplative practices and their relevance to professions in general and education in particular.

Miller, J. (1996/2001). *The holistic curriculum.* Toronto: University of Toronto Press.

This text presents a framework for holistic education and explores various practices through the concept of connectedness.

Miller, J. (2000). *Education and the soul: Toward a spiritual curriculum.* Albany: SUNY Press.

The concept of soul is explored and how soul can be nurtured in educational settings.

Miller, J., Karsten, S., Denton, D., Orr, D., & Colallilo Kates, I. (2005). *Holistic learning and spirituality in education.* Albany: SUNY Press.

This book includes a collection of papers on holistic education from a series of conferences held at the Ontario Institute for Studies in Education at the University of Toronto. Authors include Rachael Kessler, Thomas Moore, Riane Eisler, and Anna Lemkow.

Miller, R. (1997). *What are schools for? Holistic education in American culture.* Brandon, VT: Holistic Education Press.

Ron Miller is one of the major figures in holistic education. Here he explores the history of holistic education as well as the current challenges that face holistic educators.

Miller, R. (2000). *Caring for new life: Essays on holistic education.* Brandon, VT: Foundation for Educational Renewal.

Miller covers a variety of topics but within a coherent vision of holistic education as he addresses both theoretical and practical issues.

Nakagawa, Y. (2000). *Education for awakening: An eastern approach to holistic education.* Brandon, VT: Foundation for Educational Renewal.

Yoshiharu Nakagawa, a professor at Rietsumeiken University in Kyoto, is one of the leading figures in holistic education. This book presents a comprehensive theoretical framework for holistic education based on Eastern thought, particularly Buddhism.

Nava, R. G. (2001). *Holistic education: A pedagogy of universal love.* Brandon, VT: Foundation for Educational Renewal.

Ramon Gallegos Nava, a holistic educator from Mexico, has written a book that has universal appeal as he presents his ideas in a clear and coherent manner. It provides an excellent overview of holistic education.

Noddings, N. (1992). *The challenge to care in schools: An alternative approach to education.* New York: Teachers College Press.

Nel Noddings is one of the leading figures in arguing for education based on an ethic of caring. This book focuses on how this vision can be actualized in schools.

Palmer, P. (1998). *The courage to teach: Exploring the inner landscape of a teacher's life.* San Francisco: Jossey-Bass.

Parker Palmer is a pioneer in the field of spirituality in education. This book has led to teachers meeting in groups in North America to explore the relevance to their work of the ideas presented in this book.

Index

**CORWIN
PRESS**

The Corwin Press logo—a raven striding across an open book—represents the union of courage and learning. Corwin Press is committed to improving education for all learners by publishing books and other professional development resources for those serving the field of PreK–12 education. By providing practical, hands-on materials, Corwin Press continues to carry out the promise of its motto: **"Helping Educators Do Their Work Better."**